ENDORSEMENTS

"One of my most valued privileges is to read numerous manuscripts from aspiring authors who want to impact homeschool families. Once or twice in my career I have read a manuscript and realized that I have just read a blockbuster. You hold such a book in your hands."

Debi Pearl | Best-Selling Author and Homeschool Mom

"Wanda is an advocate for the power of homeschooling as well as a transparent voice on its potential pitfalls. Having been both a homeschooled child and a homeschooling parent, she brings a unique perspective and much-needed balance to the subject. If you're looking for a realistic homeschooling strategy, look no further than *Homeschool With Ease*."

Donna Partow | Best-Selling Author and Homeschool Mom

"As one of the early pioneers of the homeschool movement, I am glad to see my daughter's book, *Homeschool With Ease*, inspire a new generation of young mothers. Wanda shares many tips and practical examples for teaching children at home through normal life experiences while keeping them interested and excited. May you be encouraged with confidence that God has also equipped you to succeed in homeschooling your own children."

Janna Baer | Homeschool Mom

WANDA KINSINGER

HOME SCHOOL WITH EASE

THE BABY YEARS & BEYOND

LIFEWISE BOOKS

HOMESCHOOL WITH EASE
THE BABY YEARS & BEYOND

BY WANDA KINSINGER

Copyright © 2020 Wanda Kinsinger.
Second Printing: July 2020

Printed in the United States of America
ISBN (Print): 978-1-952247-01-9
ISBN (Ebook): 978-1-952247-02-6

All Scripture quotations are taken from the King James Holy Bible

ALL RIGHTS RESERVED. This book contains material protected under International and Federal Copyright Laws and Treaties. Any unauthorized reprint or use of this material is prohibited. No part of this book may be produced or transmitted in any form or by any means, electronic or mechanical, including photocopying, recording, or by any information storage and retrieval system without prior written permission from the author or publisher except in the case of brief quotations embodied in critical articles and reviews.

1. Homeschooling 2. Teaching 3. Children 4. Child Psychology 5. Family Home Economics 7. Religion/Spirituality 8. Family 9. Child Training 10. Adoption
I. Kinsinger, Wanda II. *Homeschool With Ease: The Baby Years & Beyond*

Published by:
LIFEWISE BOOKS
PO BOX 1072
Pinehurst, TX 77362
LifeWiseBooks.com

To contact the author | wandakinsinger.com

DEDICATION

To my Papa God, whose faithfulness in my life has never wavered, who has always been by my side: loving me, leading me, teaching me, and training me, even when I didn't realize it. It is His goodness that has brought me to where I am today and to the completion of this book. He helped me when I thought I couldn't go on. It is His parenting example that gave me insight, wisdom, and encouragement with my own children. This book is for His glory.

ACKNOWLEDGEMENTS

Joy, you believed in me and encouraged me. You had more faith in me than I did in myself. Thanks for your patient help in organizing the book outline. Here's the final product—a real printed book written by your mom. Enjoy!

Jesse and Joy, thank you for the many meals, extra chores, and practical help around the house that gave me time to write.

James, thank you for the daily phone calls from college and your encouragement, support, and listening to my progress reports.

John, thank you for keeping me covered in prayer as I underwent the writing process. This book has been covered and written in prayer.

Marrita Thompson, you were an answer to prayer. Thanks for the encouragement, support, and feedback you provided, as well as the subtitle idea.

Donna Partow and Tamera Aragon, thanks for your wisdom and perseverance with me during the "7 Days to Freedom" events.

Those weeks changed the trajectory of my life and started me down this journey towards becoming an author.

Charity Bradshaw, a million thanks. This book would have remained in the womb and never been born without your expertise in the "labor" process.

LifeWise Books Team, thanks to each one of you for your help through the editing and publishing process, and assisting in the final stages of making this book a reality.

CONTENTS

Introduction	I
Chapter 1: Homeschool Kid to Homeschool Mom	1
Chapter 2: Dropping the Age Expectations—& Pressure!	11
Chapter 3: Raising Responsible Learners	25
Chapter 4: Be Purposeful ... On Purpose	37
Chapter 5: Be a Student of Your Child	47
Chapter 6: Own the Atmosphere	57
Chapter 7: How to Create Interest for Learning	67
Chapter 8: Wonders of the Whiteboard	79
Chapter 9: Practice with Everyday Learning	101
Chapter 10: Personalized Curriculum, Grading, & Testing	109
Chapter 11: Meeting Your Goals	127
Practical Tips & Ideas: Creative Teaching in Daily Life	133
Works Cited	213
About the Author	217
Connect with Wanda	218

Practical Tips & Ideas: Creative Teaching in Daily Life   133

    Phonics & Reading   134

    Handwriting & Early Grammar   151

    Spelling & Vocabulary   157

    Verbal & Speech Skills   166

    Mathematics   168

    Finances & Stewardship   187

    Science, Biology, & Health   193

    History, Geography, & Economics   199

    Scripture: Study & Memorization   206

INTRODUCTION

I am a product of homeschooling. My parents were among the first few of the homeschool movement in the 1980s. They were told by friends and family that they would ruin our lives, we'd never get into college, and we'd end up socially handicapped. I'm here to say that none of those things happened to us.

Quite the opposite occurred. Each of my siblings and I attended college and thrived in our career choices. We chose auto mechanics and real estate, physical therapy, veterinary technician, horticulture, dental assistant, and music teacher.

I have had the privilege and opportunity to be both a homeschool kid and a homeschool mom. It is from these experiences that I write this book. Both experiences were vastly different, yet both held many "homeschool" similarities.

As a homeschool kid, I know the joys of homeschool flexibility and opportunity. As a homeschool mom, I also know the realities of the responsibility, time, and effort it takes each day to make it happen.

I also understand the frustrations, self-doubts, and emotional drain that comes along with schooling at home. I know what it's like to wonder about and question my own ability to school my children successfully and keep them on target. My goal was to properly prepare them to independently launch into their own futures. Could I do it?

Yes, I could! And you can, too.

That's what this book is about. I believe anyone can homeschool and do it well. One does not need to hold a teaching certificate in order to do so. God created you with everything you need to raise your child in every way. He also tells us how to do this in ways that matter and are most effective. In addition, with all the resources available today, it is even easier to homeschool than what I experienced.

My goal for this book is to expose the myths and unreasonable expectations that are out there, to lessen the sense of overwhelm about learning and homeschooling in general, and to provide encouragement and ideas for creative teaching in all subjects.

It is my prayer that by reading this book, you will experience a renewed hope, confidence, and reassurance in your abilities to school your children at home. I'd love to know that what I've shared and the examples I've given will stir up your own inspiration and creativity.

Above all, I pray that this book expels the fears of homeschooling, removes any doubt about your qualifications, and equips you with tools and ideas for your own successful and fun journey toward learning.

I hope you enjoy reading this as much as I enjoyed writing it.

Blessings,

Wanda Kinsinger

CHAPTER 1
HOMESCHOOL KID TO HOMESCHOOL MOM

I was born and raised in rural Illinois. I was the second of six children. Four of us were close in age, with two younger sisters born several years later. We were part of the farming community, attended church regularly, and enjoyed the country life growing up. In my earlier memories, I attended a little country school for my first three years of education. My class was the largest, at thirteen students. The smallest class consisted of only four students. Except for kindergarten, two grades shared a room with one teacher.

During my third-grade year, my parents moved about ten miles south, putting us into a much larger school district. With two youngsters in the car, my mother shuttled my older brother and me back and forth to school each day to finish out the school year.

BECOMING A HOMESCHOOL KID

Early that summer we learned that we were going to start homeschooling. My younger sister would be starting kindergarten, so Mom started out with my brother in fourth grade, me in third grade, my sister as a kindergartner, and a preschooler.

I'm not sure what options were available to my parents at that time, but they chose to homeschool correspondence-style through a Christian school who provided this service to missionaries and international families. This method was more rigid, with specific book requirements and schoolwork deadlines. But it also afforded my mom with assistance in grading, testing, and report cards.

We went through initial placement testing and were sent the curriculum books. Oh, what excitement filled the house when the box of new books arrived! We were so eager to get started that we didn't wait until fall but got started on our new books right away. I reveled in the new freedoms and opportunities that lay before me.

As autumn rolled around, I could read my assignments, do my work, finish early, and be outside playing, long before the school bus drove past in the afternoon. As I began to experience the newfound benefits of homeschooling, the possibilities seemed endless. I became self-paced and worked my school schedule around desired activities, hobbies, and outings. By fifth grade, I was helping to create my personalized school schedule, and by seventh grade I was fully in charge of my own schedule. I loved the freedom I had to be flexible. I was able to set my own "hours" and choose my days off. I took advantage of this flexibility to spend time with friends, help out on the farm, and accept odd jobs elsewhere.

GRADUATING EARLY

It didn't take me long to realize that I did not need an entire school year to complete each required grade level, and the desire to graduate early was born. I already had a head start and was very motivated. I wanted to graduate two years early but was given permission for only one year. My father did not want me to graduate ahead of my older brother. Since I had "extra" time, I took the opportunity to work outside the home whenever possible, accepting babysitting jobs during normal school hours.

At fifteen, I attended driver's education at our district's public school. After getting my license, I took classes at a community college and received my nursing assistant certificate. School generally took me about four hours to complete. I was finished by noon on most days, so I began working second shift at a nursing home.

Even with a full-time job, I met my goal and graduated a year early. I was accepted directly into the physical therapy program at our local college, though the program only accepted six students directly from high school, with everyone else on a ten-year waiting list.

Each of my siblings' education paths looked different from mine. My older brother chose to finish his last two years of high school at public school. My following two siblings homeschooled all their years, graduated on time, then went straight to college. My youngest two sisters experienced a combination of homeschool, private school, and public school. None of us had any trouble getting into college. No one guessed we were homeschooled unless we mentioned it. Once in college we were the "same" as every other high school student.

BEING A HOMESCHOOL MOM

When I was nineteen, I graduated from therapy school during one weekend and got married the next. A couple of years later we adopted our first of three babies from Vietnam. When our son was three years old, we welcomed home another son and a daughter, who were seven months and five months old at the time. Though they were only two months apart, they were different in everything. We had our hands full. It was like having twins, except that they were *not* twins. Those two months have always mattered immensely between the two of them. This unique age difference played a huge part in our parenting, their schooling, and their own decisions while growing up.

When our oldest was approaching kindergarten, my husband lost his job and we underwent a role reversal. I went back to work and he became Mr. Mom while getting an online bachelor's degree. My husband had not had a great public school experience and wanted our children to be homeschooled. So while he did his own classwork, he homeschooled our oldest for the next three years.

Since I was most familiar with the correspondence-type homeschooling that my parents used, that is what we started with. It also seemed more streamlined for my husband to follow. After receiving his bachelor's degree, my husband was offered a job internationally and we moved to Asia for the next three years.

LIVING IN A FOREIGN COUNTRY

I began homeschooling the younger two while living in Asia. They were six years old and nearly opposites in everything from personalities to learning preferences. Because of these considerable differences, I decided not to use any formal curriculum with them until the first grade. I needed time to figure out how I would try to approach teaching them together in a way that met each of their needs.

While my youngest child could sit contentedly and focus for hours, my middle child couldn't sit still, had a short attention span, hated to write, and in general held a strong resistance towards academics. Since they were both in the same grade, how could I reach both of them effectively?

Just as important, how did I support the younger to excel while encouraging the older to do his best without inflaming the constant self-comparisons between the two? The children's self-image, integrity, and character were at stake. Both were very bright and intelligent. However, my middle child suffered for years with adoption issues that took us a long time to learn about and address.

While my youngest was bold, confident, and outgoing, my middle son felt insecure, insignificant, and lacked self-assurance. I did not want to add to his personal struggles by applying any academic pressure that would strengthen the misconceptions he held about himself.

● ● ● ● ● ● ● ● ● ● ●

I learned early on that homeschooling children meant more than just the three R's. It encompasses the whole child, their perceptions, and their outlook on life.

● ● ● ● ● ● ● ● ● ● ●

When they were six and a half, the day came when both children were begging to learn to read. My daughter had been asking for a while, but now my son was also expressing his desire to read. They already knew their letters and sounds. Since they were both motivated, they began reading in under two weeks. It was quick and painless. All my children became avid readers. Because of our experience, we concluded that "later is better."

This became my homeschooling attitude: *Wait a little longer until the child is ready and then learn something quickly.* It was far better than pushing something earlier and putting both parties through unnecessary pain and frustration. So I waited. This was especially true for my son.

As for the other subjects, I got quite creative, since there was very little available to me in a foreign country. I used coloring books. I made my own flash cards and laminated them. I went online and we would google things. I bought and hung a whiteboard. As much as possible, I incorporated all learning styles—visual, auditory, and kinesthetic.

BACK IN AMERICA

After we returned to the United States, the children became very interested in attending public school. They were all middle school age at the time, going into the eighth and fifth grades. It was often the topic of conversation at the dinner table. I struggled a bit on my end. It felt a bit like failure and rejection that the kids didn't want to continue being homeschooled. I had loved homeschooling. Why didn't they?

I came to two conclusions. There comes a time when you need to respect the child's decisions. Sometimes it is better to have peace in the home than strife. In this situation, I understood that there are always pros and cons to everything. Nothing is all positive or all negative. It is what we value and how we handle these situations that shapes our outlook, responses, and experiences.

My husband and I put the ball in their court. We carefully laid out the pros and cons and allowed them to make their individual schooling choices. The boys were most eager to go to public school, and my daughter didn't want to be left out. Their final decisions were to all attend public middle school.

Though the children began receiving their academic learning outside the home, I still operated in the home from a place of teaching. I kept watching for teachable moments, pointing out life applications and continuing to focus on their integrity, character, and value as an individual. It was still my job to make learning meaningful, both academically and otherwise.

When a child came home with a complaint about a teacher or a class, I'd listen and ask questions to clarify and understand. I was often able to make real life applications about why it mattered to learn such "nonsense." In addition, I would point out that in real life as an adult, they may not always see eye to eye with others but may find themselves in a position to submit to authority anyway. In such situations, their attitude could be of more consequence than the disputed matter. I applied this to their teachers and told them there were no grounds for disrespect, regardless if they were right. I would share ideas about how to respectfully approach a person in authority.

So I continued with the heart of homeschool and taught life applications to my children in reference to school. Though I didn't hold an active role with curriculum during those years, I never gave up my responsibility as primary teacher to my children.

HIGH SCHOOL YEARS

As they entered high school, the playing field began to change again. My oldest son became fascinated with becoming a doctor and neurosurgeon, so I challenged him to become a CNA (certified nursing assistant) first. During the summer that he turned sixteen, he did so and loved it. In fact, when it came time for school to start again, he didn't want to go to high school.

He wanted to homeschool again so he could continue working. Having had a taste of a real job, money, and the adult life, he was done with high school. He wanted to graduate as soon as possible. And so he did…a year and a half early. He attended a community college for a semester before transferring out of state to undergraduate school for pre-med studies.

In seventh grade, my daughter also chose to return to homeschooling. She loved math at public school but was not being challenged in it. She chose to switch all her subjects to homeschool except band, which she continued with for the following year. She also made it her goal to graduate two years early, which she did, even as she was building her own business.

She turned sixteen the same month she graduated, and then she headed off to college. She made the Dean's list her first semester and was at the top in her math class. Then she decided to switch to online schooling for computer coding and programming, an intense curriculum which she completed in nine months, thrusting her into the real world of computers and electronics.

My middle son's choice to stay in public school and graduate on time—class of 2020—remained constant. It wasn't easy having his younger sister graduate ahead of him, and we had many talks. It was a journey of character-building toward acceptance. He came to realize that his choice was not a reflection of his abilities but a personal decision. As of this writing, he is wrapping up his senior year, content to graduate on time and begin moving into his own future.

CONCLUSIONS OF MY HOMESCHOOL JOURNEY

● ● ● ● ● ● ● ● ● ●

I have learned from my experiences as a homeschool kid and a homeschool mom: Anyone can homeschool.

● ● ● ● ● ● ● ● ● ●

It may just look different for everyone. My mom often said, "I knew up to third grade when we started homeschooling. After that, I learned one grade with each child."

My mom pushed us to know more and go further than she did. She didn't homeschool us based on her knowledge, but based on the belief that, given the opportunity, we could far excel her. And she made us responsible for our own learning.

I built on those basics and added details for a more personalized approach. I didn't want my children experiencing the same pain in learning that I had initially encountered. I also knew very early on that I needed to take into account the different learning styles and personality differences that my youngest two presented by being in the same grade.

In the younger years, it's about how you approach learning and teaching. As they get older and exceed your level, it's built on the foundation that's already been laid for them to be responsible for their own learning.

If you can read and you know basic math, you can learn whatever you need to know in order to homeschool successfully. Be a learner, and learn with your children. Often, as I taught I learned something new each time. Sometimes it was curricular, and sometimes it was about how my children learned the content, which helped me adjust my teaching styles.

I encourage you not to worry about what you don't know. You can either learn it or find someone who does know. Just be a willing student yourself. It's really about attitude.

CHAPTER 2
DROPPING THE AGE EXPECTATIONS—& PRESSURE!

I love words. I love spelling games and contests, especially spelling backwards. I love playing on the meaning and sounds of words. I thoroughly enjoy working with grammar, conjugation, and composition. And diagramming? The longer the sentence, the better. My mom told me that I should be an English teacher. One would never know I had such a rocky start in this subject!

A PAINFUL LEARNING EXPERIENCE

My earliest memories of reading and comprehension were distressing. I remember sitting with my mom, painstakingly sounding out single letters, struggling with blends. It was a mountain to slowly conquer, one three-letter word after another, until reaching the end of a one-lined sentence like, "The big fat cat sat on the hat." The most difficult were the *E* sentences like, "The hen set the egg in the nest."

"What did you read?" Mom would ask. I had no clue. I'd look at the pictures and try to guess what the sentence might have been about. When I got it wrong, it was back to the painful process of sounding out and re-reading the sentence. This became a repeated scene in our house, one that was extremely unpleasant for both my mother and me, and it usually ended with her giving up in frustration and me running away in tears.

I was in first grade, and apparently not picking up reading quickly enough at school for the teacher's satisfaction. She sent home practice books in order for my mom to give me additional practice. I endured countless sessions of brain torture, and I experienced massive hits to my self-confidence over it. I sure was glad that, by second grade, I was neck-and-neck to being top math student in my small class of thirteen!

Even after switching to homeschool, my comprehension levels continued to trail far behind normal. I usually bombed the reading and comprehension placement tests. I dreaded paragraphs. The longer the paragraph, the worse it was. It was a sea of words that jumbled horribly in my mind. There were too many words at once to make any sense. I usually picked a couple of target words from a paragraph when I needed to answer questions about it. Needless to say, I often failed those questions. I continued to struggle so badly in this area that I gave up believing I'd ever comprehend well. I hated reading and couldn't imagine anyone doing it for pleasure.

However, during the summer between my fourth and fifth grade, something happened. When I hit the books that fall, I effortlessly understood everything I was reading! It was like a whole new world opened up to me. I began to read books with an unquenchable thirst. Soon my mother was complaining about me being a bookworm and not getting my chores done. I couldn't imagine anyone *not* loving to read. My self-confidence returned and I thrived in my subjects.

My love for reading and learning only grew from that point on. My most enjoyed subject became English and composition. By eighth grade, I was in a senior-level book, and by my junior year, I completed a sophomore college-level book. By my senior year, much to my dismay, the homeschool curriculum could not provide any higher-level book and I was placed back to a high school level book that year. It was awful and boring.

LABELING

My husband also experienced difficulty in his early learning years. His was a different story, though. Long before learning styles were recognized and acknowledged, those who didn't learn by traditional methods were often labeled. Between his third and fourth summer, he was placed in a remedial class with those who were less advanced than what was considered normal for their ages. The labeling effect this had on my husband's self-image, confidence, and view of himself affected him for years afterward. Though he learned to read during the following year, he continued to carry the stigma of having a learning disability.

These are two similar learning difficulties, two very different outcomes. Since learning my husband's story, I've often wondered if I would have been labeled and how different my story would have turned out if I had experienced what he did. And what his story might have looked like if he'd had the time without labeling like I did. What this impressed upon me was a deep belief.

> **Every child deserves the freedom to learn at their own pace.**

Not pressed to meet someone else's parameters of "normal," but to have the freedom to learn when they are ready, without judgement. This belief played a huge role in how I homeschooled my children. From my own experience, I knew that brains "clicked" at different times and rates, and from my husband's experience, I realized that how it was handled affected self-perception and self-confidence. Perception is easily misconstrued and not easily undone. Especially self-perception. And self-perception is directly linked to confidence.

BEHIND, ON SCHEDULE, OR AHEAD?

A common question that plagues mothers, especially those who homeschool is, "Is my child behind, on schedule, or ahead?" We mothers start worrying and comparing our children from birth. Can he hold up his head yet? When did he start to crawl? Is he walking yet? Has he lost his first tooth? As they grow, these concerns give way to new ones. Do they know their ABC's? Can they write their name? Can they read? And then we hear comments that make us wonder... Is he getting what he needs in high school? Is he prepared for college? Will he succeed in life?

We want the best for our children, and in defining what that is, we often look around and compare our child to others. Sometimes, we take on pride when we see that our child is ahead of most others his age. Or, we may feel embarrassed when our child seems to be a bit behind. These attitudes are detrimental to the child. They catch on to our expectation levels and can become discouraged, picking up a no-care attitude, or going into pretense trying to satisfy us. Neither are good or healthy.

Because of the scars from my past learning experiences, I refused to be swayed by popular "normals" and put pressure on my children. I knew there had to be a better way, and I was willing to take the risk to find it. I got many peculiar looks when I didn't appear concerned that my youngest two were six years old and had not yet begun to read.

"Aren't you worried that they'll be behind?" I was asked.

"Not at all," I responded. But they didn't know how to handle my lack of concern.

● ● ● ● ● ● ● ● ●

The truth is, "when" DOES matter, but not like most think.

● ● ● ● ● ● ● ● ●

Waiting may be the kindest gift you give your young child. Don't allow bragging rights, pride, or satisfaction to overrule your good sense. Your child's self-image is worth more than your pride.

STOP COMPARING

You know your child best. Be sure you are not pushing or pressuring him in order to keep up appearances or satisfy others' expectations. It's not *when* they learn it that matters, it's *how* and *that* they learn it; and learn it well.

Let yourself and your child off the hook from mainstream expectations and pressures that bring insecurity and stress. Worry less about measuring up to either the public school or the homeschool "standard." Homeschool is a different dynamic than public school, so don't try to follow the public-school template. And don't worry about what others will think. Each family operates differently. Trying to operate like another family with what works for them will only bring you grief and failure. Stop comparing yourself. As with all comparisons, someone falls short, and that party is most often yourself.

You are unique, your family is unique. Respect those differences. Honor your child's individual development time frame and learning curve. You'll both be glad you did.

WAITING UNTIL THEY ARE READY

As a child, my middle son already exhibited low levels of self-confidence, so I entered the arena of schooling with caution and great care. He was already sensitive to the fact that his younger

DROPPING THE AGE EXPECTATION—& PRESSURE!

sister of two months was pulling at the bit and wanting to start school. He compared himself to her and decided that he was not as smart. He was ready to throw in the towel before he began. Rather than push him into something he was not mentally prepared to handle (though academically able), I waited. I decided to focus on learning in real life, not the books. I figured that peer pressure would do its work, and curiosity would give it a boost.

I was right. I did not apply pressure, and seemingly didn't care. It was only a matter of time before he wanted to learn to read. That's when both he and his sister learned to read in under two weeks. From this experience, I knew my theory had substance: *wait a little longer, then it's a much quicker and less painful process.* This cycle was repeated many times during my years of homeschooling.

● ● ● ● ● ● ● ● ●

It's easier on both mom and child to start later with peace than earlier with stress and strife.

● ● ● ● ● ● ● ● ●

What plagued my son was fear of failure. He had to arrive at the point of believing in himself before he took the risk to learn. When I waited and then he learned quickly, I was able to capitalize on that success for the next hurdle.

One of my ongoing job descriptions with him in both life and school has been to speak encouragement to him and confirm my confidence in his abilities. It never would have helped to pressure him before he was ready. Your child is unique, and he *will* learn on his timetable if you are patient and support him rather than push and prod him. This is a beautiful liberty that homeschooling affords. Take advantage of its offer.

When you don't push subject matter before they are ready, you save yourself and your child a headache or two, or ten. Kids catch up far more quickly than we give them credit for. What locks up the brakes is when your child picks up on your stress and anxiety levels. So relax! Allow your child to enjoy school instead of dreading it.

RELEASE THE PRESSURE: THE ONE-ON-ONE EFFECT

Did you know that one day with you can be equal to several days in a classroom? The fact that your ratio of 1:1 teacher to student is powerful. Take for example a class of twenty or thirty. The teacher spends a week teaching new material. The following week, she gives a test and finds that most of the class did not properly understand the concept. She must then spend a few more days reviewing the subject and re-testing before moving on.

This teacher cannot possibly give each child the one-on-one attention needed in order to know if each child is understanding the material, but you can. In fact, in a short amount of time, you can discover that you need to change up the teaching style or explain something again in another way. You have the advantage of time because you hold the advantage of one-on-one teaching. If your child is not catching on, you will know. Instead of beating a dead horse, you can let it go until tomorrow and try again without it becoming a place of stress and strife. Even if it takes a week for them to learn it, you can still be ahead.

DROPPING THE AGE EXPECTATION — & PRESSURE!

On the other hand, if they catch onto something quickly because you waited for the right time and are teaching them the way they learn best, you've just accelerated them. They might finish school early that day, or you might have some wiggle room to tackle another area up ahead that may take a little more time. You can be more relaxed, knowing you've got the time. In this way you can teach on a time-flexible schedule.

CULTURAL AND SOCIAL EFFECTS

When I grew up, homeschooling was legal but unpopular. Now it's cool to homeschool. However, in Germany, it's prohibited. In South Korea, it's unclear. Our country's laws and culture influence our attitude toward schooling and learning.

Schooling in America has changed over the past decade. By the time my children were approaching school age, there was a new push to learn more at a younger age. In our growing culture of fast food and instant gratification, faster and earlier is often being mistaken for better. Parents feel a new pressure about what their toddlers are learning.

Anne Stoudt, a kindergarten teacher in suburban New Jersey for 19 years, says, "Kindergarten is now first grade, and first grade is now second grade. It used to be normal for first graders to still be learning to read. Now, the handful of kindergartners who aren't reading by the end of the year are considered behind."[1]

Teaching my children while living in two foreign countries challenged some of my standards and beliefs.

● ● ● ● ● ● ● ● ● ●

> I was forced to take another look,
> reconsider, and admit that sometimes
> my idea of normal was just one
> way to look at something.

● ● ● ● ● ● ● ● ● ●

Each country, culture, and community holds unique strengths and weaknesses. South Korea, Japan, and Finland all score high on international testing. However, Finland was rated by the UN in the 2018 Happiness Index as the happiest country in the world.[2] South Korea and Japan experience higher rates in teen suicide linked to the pressures of school. What makes the difference?

I've lived in both South Korea and Japan. I can testify to their excellence in education and their drive for excellence overall. They press their children to exceed themselves, often sacrificing greatly to do so. They stand by their work and have a communal pride for the accomplishments of their schools, universities, professions, and country. However, I can also testify to the stress, strain, and pressure that often accompanies the learning. High expectations are placed on those children. Many young children attend specialty and extracurricular classes before entering kindergarten. In South Korea, the older grades often remain in school until late at night to study for intense and competitive exams.

In Finland, formal schooling does not start until age seven. But by age fifteen, they outperform most countries on international assessments.[3] Finland rocked the academic world when they placed first in the international testing in 2000, and have remained in the top ten ever since. Japan and South Korea often place in the top ten consistently, as well, but the US has not placed yet in the top ten for any subject categories.[4]

After gaining the world's attention, more information came out about Finland's way of schooling. As I've become aware of Finland's educational policies, what I have found has been encouraging and supports what I have believed for years—that later is better, and learning is built on relationship with an emphasis on personal responsibility.

School in Finland is much more relaxed, with 15 minutes of recess for every 45 minutes of classroom time. This increases the students' attentiveness in class.[5] They also do not undergo routine standardized testing, but place emphasis on relationship and responsibility, life application, and a positive learning environment.[6] When children attend a kindergarten at six years old, the focus isn't on preparing them for school academically; instead the main goal is to make sure that the children are happy and responsible individuals.[7]

Finland's academic results confirm my belief:

● ● ● ● ● ● ● ● ● ●

It is good to first learn by play, lay the foundation for character, and teach responsibility in the very young years.

● ● ● ● ● ● ● ● ● ●

Then when the child is ready, build upon these basics by introducing academics with life application. Waiting until your child is ready to learn is worth the wait and does not put them behind. In fact, it may be an integral ingredient for springboarding them ahead.

So, relax, Mama. Release yourself. Cut yourself (and your kids) some slack. Increased stress levels are no fun for anyone. Reasonable school expectations will help lower those stress levels and will help everyone in the home to relax and have fun. I've included a reference for a good read about an American teacher's first year of teaching at a Finnish school, called "How Finland Starts the School Year."[8]

EARLIER OR LATER?

Along these same lines, research from the University of Otago in New Zealand has shown that children who learned to read at five and children who learned to read at seven showed no differences in their reading abilities by the time they were ten to eleven years of age.[9]

This explains my struggle with reading comprehension until the summer after I turned ten. My brain "clicked" and BINGO! I was immediately on track and excelling in the very area I'd struggled so hard in. I'm thankful I was given the time to develop without being labeled by either a teacher or my parents.

Too often, we put ourselves and our children under unnecessary pressure and stress in order to please someone else or satisfy social standards. But who defines these standards we often measure ourselves by? Whose values, whose goals, and whose expectations are leading or driving you? When you feel pressure, back up a bit and re-evaluate.

DROPPING THE AGE EXPECTATION — & PRESSURE!

Many people can have many opinions, but it is what works for you and your child that will ultimately work best for you. You know your child best. And the best teacher is the one who understands her student. The most effective mother is the one who understands her child.

Challenge your child as early as they show interest so they don't get bored. But don't push them into territory they're not ready for. This can easily and needlessly discourage them. It's okay if they are ahead in some things and need some additional time in others. Give them a few years and the differences will diminish. Rest assured that what you are teaching them will eventually all come together.

It may take some courage to take a stand and be different. But I have learned that different is not always wrong or bad. It can be just different. And sometimes different can challenge our own standards to become better. There are many things I learned while living in Asia that affected my parenting and schooling habits. Some of their ways I loved, and others I learned from.

WHEN LATER IS BETTER

While we lived in Asia, I struggled with how to teach and demonstrate gallons, quarts, and cups in the midst of a metric world of liters and grams. How could I make it meaningful? Well, I really couldn't. So, I skipped that part in the book and told the kids we'd come back to it.

When we returned to the States, it didn't bother me that my kids were well past the age of learning their measurements. I didn't immediately push to catch them up, either. I let them adjust and watched for a natural opening. When the opportunity for measuring liquids presented itself, I took advantage of it.

In one day, the kids effortlessly learned both their measurements and conversions. They'd already learned how to multiply and divide, so it was a quick study. Afterwards, I brought out the math book from two years prior and they had fun answering the questions…it was so easy now. Perception is everything.

Once again, I solidified my conclusion that waiting until kids were more than ready and capable made it easier for all involved. It also helped to avoid unnecessary strife and fighting with the child to learn. If something isn't "clicking" when you introduce a subject, don't worry or stress out. Leave it for another day, week, or month. Your child WILL "click" and, in that moment, may make up 6 months' worth in just days.

By choosing to wait, I was able to make learning measurements meaningful, applicable to their cultural experience, and easy since they already knew multiplication and division. They didn't suffer from not knowing these measurements two years earlier, and they retained the knowledge after just an hour of play-practice.

CHAPTER 3
RAISING RESPONSIBLE LEARNERS

The biggest part and most critical factor of homeschooling is your home life. It's first about lifestyle and attitude, not curriculum. It's important to instill foundational values upon which the knowledge of curriculum can be built. The best curriculum in the world cannot substitute a lack of appreciation for learning or the self-discipline to receive instruction. Proverbs 1:7 says, "The fear of the LORD is the beginning of knowledge: but fools despise wisdom and instruction."

These character strengths are built during home life, not while the child is sitting at a desk or table doing his homework. In fact, that home life will determine *how* he sits and does his homework. Will he accept instruction or resist it?

BIBLICAL GUIDANCE TO TEACHING

"Whom shall he teach knowledge? and whom shall he make to understand doctrine? them that are weaned from the milk, and drawn from the breasts. For precept must be upon precept, precept upon precept; line upon line, line upon line; here a little, and there a little:" (Isaiah 28:9-10)

From the time we are babies and throughout our lives, we learn best by building one precept (command or rule) upon another. We learn a little here and a little more there. None of us wants to sit down to a whole new concept, be expected to learn it and get tested on it shortly afterwards. If the idea is not foreign to us, if it's something we've already become familiar with, it's not so hard to learn something a little more specific with detailed instructions about it. We might even be interested in doing so.

● ● ● ● ● ● ● ● ● ●

Long before introducing a new topic in school, I would introduce it in life.

● ● ● ● ● ● ● ● ● ●

"And these words, which I command thee this day, shall be in thine heart: and thou shalt teach them diligently unto thy children, and shalt talk of them when thou sittest in thine house, and when thou walkest by the way, and when thou liest down, and when thou risest up. And thou shalt bind them for a sign upon thine hand, and

they shall be as frontlets between thine eyes. And thou shalt write them upon the posts of thy house, and on thy gates." (Deuteronomy 6:6-9)

Teaching is a full-time job. Teaching doesn't wait and apply only during school hours. When teaching according to the above verse is diligently applied, school takes place at all hours, in all places. The great thing about this is that at any time you can use something you notice to your advantage and create a learning moment right then, laying the groundwork towards a topic you want to introduce or build upon later.

A side benefit of this habit is that I never heard the complaint, "Mom, we're not in school right now!" My kids knew I'd use any teachable moment I could. In fact, I even took advantage of the time they'd use in the bathroom by posting things on the door, on the wall across from the toilet, on the mirror, etc.

"Train up a child in the way he should go: and when he is old, he will not depart from it." (Proverbs 22:6)

I invested a lot of time and effort into training my children to become responsible human beings: for themselves, their own decisions, and their own learning. I wanted them to be responsible *for* themselves, *to* others, and *before* God.

By accomplishing this, I have given my children a great gift for life. Young adults who have a healthy respect for the gravity and meaning of life, yet also hold a sense of self-confidence, are well prepared to successfully launch out into their own lives.

BUILDING BASIC VALUES

I knew the values and attitudes I wanted to instill in my children and knew it was my own responsibility to demonstrate each one first if I were to expect it from them later. I understood that my own attitude would make a difference. I would need to think ahead in order to help my children be prepared for what they may encounter in life. I started with the basics of honesty, integrity, and character, and then added curiosity, love of learning, self-discipline, and delayed gratification, all in the context of relationship and life.

Before my children were old enough to talk, I taught them sign language for simple words like please, thank you, water, toilet, hungry, all done, and other such essentials in toddler vocabulary. I'd make the sign each time I said the word. Then, each time they signed, I responded to them. When they signed "thank you," I signed and answered, "You are very welcome!" with a smile. If they signed the need for the water, I'd ask, "How do you ask?" and show them how to combine "water" with "please" as I said, "May I have some water, please?"

I consistently signed and spoke with them in this manner, so when they began to speak, it was natural for them to begin talking this way. Out in public there was always amazement expressed when a one-year-old told them thank you without prompting, or said, "Yes, please," when offered something.

As they built their vocabulary, I addressed the truth of their words. If I asked a question and they told a lie, I would carefully and clearly separate out the consequence I was giving for what they did wrong versus the lie they had told. The consequence for lying was always greater. Sometimes what they'd done was simply a teachable moment, not a disciplining one. Then, I would only add the consequence for the lie afterwards. They picked up quickly that it was less painful to tell the truth than to get caught in a lie.

Next, I addressed the importance of keeping their word. If they said something, I held them to it. I made sure that I only said what I meant, as well. This is crucial if you want your children to trust your word and believe what you say. How can they take you seriously if you do not take your own words seriously?

Along with words is the importance of following up with action. If not, words are useless, and over time become meaningless. If a child was misbehaving, I would tell them what I would do if they didn't obey. "Do not hit your sister with that toy or I will take it away for the rest of the day."

If he chooses to hit again, I do not have to get angry. I calmly carry out my word. If he cries, I remind him that he chose to disobey. The child still had his choice in the matter, and I kept my word in return.

• • • • • • • • • •

> Children must have an honest and clear choice in their behavior if they are going to learn to be responsible for their own decisions.

• • • • • • • • • •

With consistency over time, the child learns to think about his actions, the consequences that follow, and the reality of his own choice. If I yelled at him to stop hitting his sister and then forcibly took the toy away, I am removing his opportunity to make a choice. That is being a bully. And sadly, it results in rebellious anger and a heart desire to retaliate.

What mattered most to me was my children's heart and attitude. Yes, even more than the actual infraction. I disciplined accordingly. My own attitude while doing so was a point of integrity I was demonstrating for them, as well. To expect more out of them than I was doing myself would be hypocrisy. When I blew it, I was quick to acknowledge it, share what I should have done, and ask their forgiveness.

THE GIFT OF WORK

My children began helping around the house long before it was work to them. Every young child wants to do what their mommy is doing, but not every mother will let them do it until they are older and "more capable." Unfortunately, often by the time they are willing to allow the child to help, the child is no longer interested. Then, it just looks like undesirable work.

Children are curious little creatures. And just like us adults, they hold the need to feel a sense of accomplishment in order to gain a sense of satisfaction for their day. When you help them meet this basic human need, it starts a pattern of curiosity, practicing, achievement, and satisfaction. This is exactly the pattern you want to encourage, for it will support their success for a lifetime.

Practically, they learn how to do things while thinking it was their idea, and they find it fun and gratifying. They enjoy the accomplishment of "work," since it is pleasurable to them. This is a mindset, and one that is important to cultivate and encourage. It later leads to a hardworking, trustworthy, respectful, and responsible young adult who is mature, respectful, and willing to learn.

Relationship-wise, it fosters a sweeter fellowship between the two of you. They feel good about themselves, and you were the one to help them. You become their hero, their cheerleader, and their advocate. You help them do what they couldn't do alone. You spur them on to new heights and greater victories.

Yes, including your child when they are being more of a hindrance, getting in your way, taking up your time, and too young to be of much help is at first a sacrifice. Or is it? Sure, I could have gotten things done much more quickly without my children's "help." But I learned that rather than being a sacrifice, it is actually an investment into the future, and it pays in huge returns.

BUSY "WORKING"

I remember my first experience with my oldest son before he was two years old. He was watching me empty the dishwasher and thought it looked so fun. He wanted to help. He was too small to reach and put much away, so I lifted him up on a stool in front of the silverware drawer.

After removing the larger sharp knives, I placed the silverware rack from the dishwasher onto the counter in front of him. I showed him where each item went, the regular spoons, the soup spoons, the small forks, the big forks, and the butter knives. He was impatient to do it "all himself." Sound familiar? I kept a watchful eye on him as I continued to put away the rest of the dishwasher load.

As we were "working" together, my husband came home from work. Surprised to see our son at the counter, my husband asked him, "What are you doing?"

"I'm *busy*," was our son's emphatic and satisfied reply. I suddenly realized how many times he'd heard me say, "Mommy's busy right now." He was so proud and pleased to be found "busy" like Mommy. I lost my job of emptying the silverware after that. It was his sacred and privileged duty to the household.

It wasn't long before he was demanding increased privileges to the knives. I decided that rather than try to keep them off-limits to an increasingly mobile toddler, it was better to teach him early. So, his first wielding of the knife was with a butter knife on a banana. Then on a sandwich. Next was a paring knife. By the time he was four, he nearly gave little old ladies heart attacks as he sliced and chopped with regular kitchen knives.

So, it was no stretch that helping with meal prep, cooking, and baking followed. Add to this laundry, sweeping, mopping, cleaning, and dusting. Each started as he expressed interest and before it became a "chore." And each one, we first did together. As he proved himself capable, I allowed him more responsibility and freedom.

If you find yourself guilty of waiting until your child can actually be helpful, you're not too late to start right where they are. Children of all ages are interested in doing what they are too young for. Start watching for your child's interest and feed into it. Use questions to capture their interest. (I expand on this in Chapter 7.) Then be prepared to allow them to fail without judgement or condemnation, as they learn to persevere toward success.

PRECEPT UPON PRECEPT

As we worked, I taught, and we had fun. There are so many lessons to be learned, just waiting to be pointed out at a teachable moment. As I taught how to measure the laundry detergent, I taught both the practical (mathematical measurement) and the concept of being a good steward (by not pouring in too much, as this always seemed to be the temptation.)

When I taught how to fry eggs, I explained sequencing and science (why we need butter in the pan first), safety and responsibility (the sensibility of cracking the eggs in a bowl first to ensure they didn't serve eggshells), and the concept of time (cook for one minute on medium heat, then turn down to low until finished). When cleaning, mopping, and dusting, I demonstrated excellence in doing a good job, however big or small.

• • • • • • • • • • • •

Habits, patterns, and routines were being formed during these activities in regard to how we related to each other while learning.

• • • • • • • • • • • •

I was intentional about piquing their interest, then spending time together learning about it. I was intentional with my words and attitudes in how I referred to things involving learning. I did my best to pull out the interesting, exciting, and fun elements. "Fun and easy," "super exciting," and "Isn't this neat?"

I taught them early concepts with real life, and this is where learning and meaningful reality came together. Sometimes I set the stage for something I wanted them to learn. It was never a surprise that there was always a lesson to be learned in everything. This eventually carried over toward academics and curriculum.

JAMES' 7TH BIRTHDAY SUPPER

When I asked my oldest son what he wanted to do for his seventh birthday, he said he wanted to make his own birthday supper. He was quite adamant that he wanted no help at all. He wanted to plan and do everything from start to finish himself. I wasn't sure if he would be able to pull it off, but I figured it couldn't hurt to let him give it a try. I was impressed that he wanted to serve rather than be served for his birthday, so I supported him in every way I could. After he chose his recipes, I had him check the fridge and freezer, and then make a list of ingredients he still required for his recipes. Any offers to help beyond grocery shopping were politely but firmly turned down.

The big day came. We were given clear instructions to stay out of the kitchen. We couldn't peek, and we were told to be ready for supper at his given time. First, he set the table. Then he disappeared into the kitchen. We heard all sorts of sounds coming from the kitchen, and occasionally it sounded like he was scrambling to keep up. Nevertheless, he accepted no assistance.

To this day, none of us remember all the details of what he made, except for dessert. He had told us that he was going to make a pie, all by himself, homemade crust and all. The type of pie would be a surprise. My sister had been practicing making apple pies—to see if "easy as pie" really was true—and my three children had been helping her with both the crust and apples. They had concluded after several pies that it really was easy as pie. Now, James wanted to try it all by himself. I told the rest of the family that it didn't matter how that pie turned out. We were all going to eat it.

Wonderful smells came from the kitchen. James came out to the dining room, filled our glasses with a drink he'd made, and had us sit down and pray. Afterwards, he served all the dishes. He had made a meat dish, a lettuce salad, a hot vegetable dish, homemade garlic bread, and applesauce. All of it was very good.

Finally, the long-awaited moment for dessert came. I held my breath as he presented his creation…a banana cream pie. I could hardly believe it. We'd never made such a pie before, and I hadn't realized he liked banana cream. Besides the crust being slightly dry from some over-kneading, it was delicious. And it was the beginning of a new family tradition.

From that birthday forward for many years, I got kicked out of the kitchen on each of my children's birthdays. The younger two didn't even wait until they turned seven. They have made all sorts of meals—from birthday breakfasts to expansive supper feasts. Sometimes they even had us dress up in our Vietnamese clothing for a cultural meal.

I share this story to point out a few important things. Much was illustrated with this meal, though we were not pushing formal academic school very hard. James organized a menu, wrote out a shopping list, prepared all the dishes, and served all the food. This alone is nowadays high school home economics.

James exhibited character traits of self-motivation, responsibility, perseverance, and dedication throughout the process. While making the meal, he demonstrated abilities with planning, critical-thinking, problem-solving, and time-management. He displayed creativity, skill, proficiency, competency, and attention to detail. And he showed evidence on paper of understanding academic concepts that he did not yet know, through his ability to follow and double the recipes.

To turn out a complete meal on time is no small feat, especially for a barely seven-year-old. This did not happen accidentally or haphazardly. It took the biblical precepts of "line upon line" and "here a little, there a little" to accomplish. Repetitive, consistent, and purposeful training. How difficult would it be then, for him to sit down and learn on paper what he already knows in reality?

• • • • • • • • • •

Raising up responsible learners comes before curriculum and is key to their continued scholastic learning.

• • • • • • • • • •

CHAPTER 4
BE PURPOSEFUL...ON PURPOSE

My top objective while teaching my children was to learn to be the least stressful and as enjoyable as possible. All while filling it with as much life application as I could provide. This goal required me to be intentional and purposeful. I had to have a teaching heart at all hours of the day, in and out of school hours. What was I teaching? How purposeful was my leading? What were my children seeing? What were they hearing?

POWER OF PARENT'S ATTITUDE

Your attitudes and beliefs make a difference with learning. It affects you as a teacher and your child as a student. You set the thermostat for learning in your home. Children follow the leader and will take their cue from you. Honoring and respectful, or grumbling and complaining; diligent and neat, or shoddy and lazy. Your own attitude matters regarding your child, his ability to learn, and your ability to teach.

The way learning is handled plays a significant role in the results. My mom's attitude was one of determination and utmost belief that her children were all capable of outperforming her. She often said, "I was a *C* student...you're all gonna do better than me." That is what she expected, and that is what she got. She believed we were bright and capable, and we lived up to it.

Children live up to their parent's standards and expectations. I grew up believing that a *C* was not acceptable. However, with the focus on higher grades, I often memorized stuff for the test just to pass. I'm sure a lot still stuck, but I wanted to highlight learning over grade levels for my own children. Especially with two children who struggled with comparing everything against each other.

The phrase my kids often heard was, "I want your best. If *C* is your best, then I'm satisfied. But if *A* is your best, then *B* is not enough." In short, I cared about their attitude, effort, and what they learned more than their final grade. Their integrity was of more value to me than their intelligence alone. And I wanted them to understand why they were learning something, not just memorizing it for the sake of a test.

● ● ● ● ● ● ● ● ● ● ●

As you introduce learning on paper and crack open the curriculum, it is important that your attitude precedes their learning.

● ● ● ● ● ● ● ● ● ● ●

As I've mentioned before, be intentional about how you speak, how you approach the topic, and how you lead with your own attitude. If you are not in a good frame of mind, it's better to wait. You set the tone and atmosphere for learning. Remember, where there is strife is every evil thing. Peace is much more effective.

TEACHING BY EXAMPLE

When I was desperately searching for help while my children were young, I heard something from a conference with Michael Pearl that impacted me and was of great encouragement. The gist of it was...

> *"If you can't do all the right things, but you can be the right person, then you can successfully raise your child."*

This simple yet profound truth influenced me throughout my children's youth, growing up, and teen years.

I have made many mistakes, but I can be the right person…

…if I can apologize quickly, repent openly to my children, and admit when I am wrong;

…if I can be grateful, quick with a smile, and verbalize to my children what I am thankful for;

…if I can be a person of my word, be careful what I say, and look for opportunities to build my children up;

…if I can see my children as the unique and amazing individuals that they are, respecting their autonomy, listening to their opinions, and hearing their ideas.

Teaching by example is the single most powerful thing you do on a daily basis. Children learn so much through osmosis. They are little sponges, always absorbing from their atmosphere. Then they mirror it back to us. We don't always like what they pick up, so it's important to remain mindful and stay focused on what we wish to teach.

Teach your children to respect you by keeping your word, enforcing it, and being trustworthy. Be the kind of person you want them to be. Only say it if you mean it, and mean what you say. Be true to your word. They must be able to believe you in order to take what you say seriously. Cultivate a trust and mutual respect between you and your child.

CONFIDENCE TOWARD LEARNING

Your confidence level toward a subject affects your child's outlook and motivation. Kids pick up on our stress and anxieties, and our attitudes alone can make a huge difference. Don't introduce a new subject until you are comfortable with it and prepared to approach it confidently. If you need some time, skip it until you're ready.

Waiting until you are mentally prepared is better than pushing into an area that you are apprehensive about. The anxious brain does not concentrate, learn, or retain as well as the happy, calm, and relaxed brain. We were created to learn and to enjoy doing so. Learning in a fun, relaxed environment is more enjoyable for both you and your child.

New topics can look terrifying or disheartening. Children need reassurance that it's not as complicated or scary as it appears. My general mode of approaching any new subject was an extra breezy attitude of, "Oh, this is easy!" If there was something they already knew the concepts of, but just didn't know what it looked like on paper, I'd say with a dismissive wave of my hand, "Piece of cake. You already know this!"

Sometimes I knew the content but was unsure of my own ability to teach some of the more complex things. Even so, I'd start off with an excited air of, "Hey, this will be easy, you'll pick it up in no time!" It was important that I speak confidently, even if I didn't always feel like it.

What would at times surprise even me was how quickly they *did* catch on. They acted according to what they believed. And they believed according to what they heard. And what they heard was the assurance of, "Hey, it's not as hard as you think it is. You can do this."

> • • • • • • • • •
> ## You must believe in their potential in order to call it forth.
> • • • • • • • • •

By approaching new topics this way, and by being purposeful in my own attitude towards even more difficult learning material, I set the atmosphere for learning. It also gave evidence to the importance and power of the spoken word.

SPEAK LIFE

Words can be powerful motivators or insurmountable barriers. Often how we approach something and what we have to say about it matters more than we realize. Our attitude, tone, and body language all play a part. Words can give us the encouragement and inspiration we need, or they can discourage and overwhelm us into paralysis.

> *"Death and life are in the power of the tongue: and they that love it shall eat the fruit thereof." (Proverbs 18:21)*

Your children need your daily, constant cheering on. They need to know that you are for them, not against them. Your child will live up to your standards, whether negative or positive. Making a firm decision ahead of time regarding what you believe about him and how you view him will determine how you will speak to him. And it matters. More than you know. One word from you can be remembered for a lifetime and drown out many other words. More times than I care to count, I've heard kids say negative things about themselves that have been spoken to them by their parents.

We humans have a habit of hanging onto destructive words, to our own detriment.

"I'm not good about..."

"I'm terrible with..."

"I stink at..."

Our world is filled with enough negative. Whether we are comparing or evaluating our learning abilities, social skills, relationship strengths, or artistic talents, we tend to believe the bad over the good. We need positive words to bring buoyancy to our spirit, soul, and lives. Your child needs to hear you speaking confidently about his abilities.

He needs to hear the assurance so he can believe it and then act upon it. When you speak truth to your child, you build their faith. There are many biblical truths you can speak into every child. This builds character, confidence, and a willingness to step out into new territory.

"So then faith cometh by hearing and hearing by the word of God." (Romans 10:17)

I often told my children, "You were created in God's image. He's creative, so you're creative." And, "God created you for a purpose, and He's given you everything you need to fulfill it." And, "You are fearfully and wonderfully made. Your brain is incredible and capable of more than you can possibly imagine. It's your job to use it responsibly."

I fully believed every word I told them and am convinced it is the truth for everyone. God has created each one of us for a purpose. We need to discover it and walk in it. Most of us are capable of so much more than we ever believe or give ourselves credit for. It's often mind-over-matter. When we believe that we can, we do. When we've been told we can't, we often don't bother to try.

BEWARE YOUR WORDS

We are all intelligent because we were created after a highly intelligent God. Everyone can learn. No one is stupid. We may make a stupid or foolish decision or mistake, but that does not make someone stupid. It is an affront to God's creativeness to call yourself or anyone else stupid. Even animals demonstrate levels of intelligence, and we were created with much more intelligence than any of them. Growing up on the farm, we even trained our turkeys.

All derogatory remarks, aimed at either ourself or another person, are often meant to hurt and belittle. Any kind of name-calling is unkind and disrespectful. The usage of many well-known phrases is degrading and often used with little thought behind them. Listen to what comes out of your mouth. Cut this type of verbiage from your vocabulary and think about what you say before you say it.

Filter your words through the Philippians 4:8 verse of "Whatsoever things are…" Remember that your children will follow your lead. How you talk about yourself towards them teaches them how to view you and how to refer to themselves. Your kids need daily reminders of who they are and who God created them to be.

"You're smart, you can do this," and "With that brain of yours, this won't take long."

I also used moments of discipline and correction to speak into their abilities. When they showed their creativity towards escaping responsibility, I would point out, "It took brains to come up with this idea. You are very bright. When you use that intelligence towards God's purpose for your life, you will be highly effective." When helpful, I would refer to these times later in school to encourage and propel them forward. "You are smart, and I know what you're capable of when you apply yourself."

CELEBRATE YOUR DIFFERENCES

As you speak into each child, never compare. Avoid any type of labeling or making comparisons. Different is not wrong or bad. We need to appreciate and value our own differences and teach our children to value the same.

One of my biggest ongoing battles was to help my youngest two appreciate their differences and value both themselves and each other. They both exhibited a very high need for challenge and competition but they responded to it in very different ways. This usually ended in their constant comparisons toward each other, each with themselves being the loser. Talk about discouraging.

Things usually came down to a misunderstanding or wrong assumption about the other that started off the fireworks. Interestingly, each party usually felt insecure and vulnerable about themselves or their own abilities. They had compared themselves to their sibling, felt that they didn't measure up, and reacted out of their disappointment. They condemned themselves to defeat where there was no need to.

They each needed an advocate who could speak into their lives to reassure them of their value, point out their strengths, and remind them how much they were loved. Jesus does this for us. We do this for our children. Your child needs you to speak God's truth to him daily. It is what gives him courage and strength.

I would tell my son, "You are an amazing young man. How God made you is incredible and unique. You were not made like your sister. God made you especially for what He needs you to do. He's created your sister for something different. It's okay that you can't do some things she does well. You have abilities that she doesn't have. God needs for you both to be different in order for each of you to accomplish the purpose He created you for." I would emphasize God's words to my daughter as well.

Speak truth and give life with your words. Your children need it. You need it. Be careful how you talk about yourself. You are speaking about a child of God. And as you speak, you teach your children how to view themselves and how to relate with others.

Be purposeful in making statements to build your children up and encourage them. They hear enough negative, even from their own thoughts, to drag them down. Comparisons kill and labels destroy. Never compare one child with another, even in your mind. Celebrate their differences and lead them to appreciate their differences as well.

CHAPTER 5
BE A STUDENT OF YOUR CHILD

God created us all differently for a reason and a purpose. That means that we will learn and perceive differently, too. That's okay. It's our job as a mother to be a student of our children. We need to learn their strengths, know their weaknesses, understand how they operate, and be familiar with their interests. In this way, we can be as effective as possible in the short years we have to prepare them for life.

LET THEIR INTERESTS BE YOUR GUIDE

Think back to when your child was an infant and toddler. What type of baby was he? Was he laid back or a go-getter? How curious or content was he? How early was he exploring and getting into stuff? How quickly did he get frustrated when he couldn't figure something out right away? How long of an attention span did he have as he built a Lego tower or as you read him a story? Did he prefer to play by himself or jump into the action with other kids?

It is important for you to be in tune to your child's learning patterns and habits. Your child is likely still learning in similar ways as he did as a baby. His personality also plays a part. Is he aggressive, laid back, impatient, curious? Watch him. You can learn a lot about how he learns by simple observation.

How does he learn how to play with a new toy? Does he ask you how it works, or does he try to figure it out himself? What kind of toys does he like? What catches his attention? Active things like balls and sports? Things that light up and play music? Stickers and fun coloring tools? What does he like to do in his free time? Activities outside, quietly looking at a book or coloring, or doing whatever you are doing?

All these and more will give you tips and insights into how your child learns. Each of your children is one of a kind. They are their own individual with a particular set of preference styles, learning styles, and personality.

They are unique in the way that they learn and relate to the world around them. They cannot be treated like their sibling, or you will hear about it. Allowing them to be different, and capitalizing on their strengths, provides them with the space they need to become their own person. They need you to support them into becoming the best version of themselves they can be.

> God personally created your child and placed him in your care with the responsibility to train him up in the way he is supposed to go.

We must take the time and effort to see our child as an individual if we are going to successfully launch her into the way God intended. If we're too busy trying to fit her into our mold or what our idea for her life looks like, we can fail to properly prepare her.

EVERYONE CAN LEARN

Everyone is born with the ability to learn. Children are all bright in their own way. They learn by different styles, different interests, and at different times, depending on brain development. But this has not always been understood. In the past, those children who learned in styles other than the norms practiced at public school were often labeled as stupid, hyperactive, difficult, or unable to learn.

When Thomas Edison was seven years old, his teacher called him addled and considered him too stupid to learn.[1] Thomas' mother knew better and began to homeschool him. Though he was dyslexic, she taught him to read, and before long he began reading every book he could get his hands on. Edison went on to invent the phonograph, incandescent light bulb, and motion picture, among a dozen other things.

Understanding learning styles is a relatively new concept. The term was coined in the 1960s and began being used in the common public by the 1980s. It is a growing field of study and research as we understand more about how the brain works and how it influences the learning process.

The three basic styles you're probably familiar with are: visual (seeing), auditory (hearing), and kinesthetic (movement). From a combination of these three, four more learning styles have been identified to help us understand how our brain can take in information and process it.

LEARNING PREFERENCES

Your child can learn from a combination of ways. Often referred to as "learning styles," such styles are not proven theory. However, we do exhibit learning *preferences,* so it is helpful to be familiar with these concepts and identify how your child best retains their learning. The most effective manner is through a combination of approaches.

I have experienced the benefits of recognizing and working with my children's learning preferences in both the teaching and the testing aspects. I noticed that a child may use a specific preference for a particular situation. I also realized the value of introducing different ways of learning. It keeps things interesting, fun, and creative. Children are capable of making improvements in their abilities and strengths using various methods of learning.

Here is a brief description of seven learning "styles" [2] (or preferences) to use as a general guide.

Visual – spatial: (picture-oriented) – Learns with images, pictures, diagrams, graphs, and color. Visual media is effective. Enjoys drawing, wants to "see it," needs to "picture it."

Auditory – musical – rhythmic: (music-oriented) – Learns with sound, music, rhyme, rhythm, and movement. Thinks best with background noise, humming, tapping a pencil, wiggling, toe-tapping, or pacing to help the thinking process.

Physical – kinesthetic: (movement-oriented) – Learns by doing, hands-on experience, and interacting with objects to learn about them. Can't sit still for long or will be fidgeting and wanting to get up and move around. Loves activities to learn.

Verbal – linguistic: (word-oriented) – Learns by reading, writing, note-taking, listening, audio, and speaking. Loves the written and spoken word. Using acronyms, rhyme, rhythm, and reading out loud helps recall.

Logical – mathematical: (logic-oriented) – Learns by numbers, equations, patterns, connections, categories, and systems. Likes logical order and examples, statistics, lists, agendas, and procedures. Wants to understand the reason behind the content being learned. Needs to know why.

Social – interpersonal: (people-oriented) – Learns by role-playing, relating to others, sharing stories, comparing ideas with others. Good communicators, verbally and non-verbally. Prefers groups or one-on-one teacher time.

Solitary – intrapersonal: (self-aware) – Learns by thinking, concentrating, and visualization. Works best when allowed to set their own goals and given the space and independence to work on their own.

Recognizing how your child learns will set you up for more effective teaching, and it will be useful to him later on as he takes responsibility for his own learning.

MAKE LEARNING MEANINGFUL / RELEVANT

One of the major keys to successful teaching is to make learning meaningful. Each piece of new information must be connected to previously held information. Connection between the two pieces of information is essential, and it is the most effective when learning is connected to your child's interests. It is critical to stay one step ahead of the inevitable question and often complaint, "What do I need to know *this* for?" The "burden of proof" is on you, Mom.

You must connect his learning to real life and do so in a way that he will understand. Be prepared for this question. I was always answering this question in my head as I was thinking about how to present a new concept. It saves a lot of time and energy, let alone pushback, answering this on the front end. For example, let's say I am preparing to introduce writing out numbers in written form. I see that soon the math book is introducing it, and I know my child needs to learn it, but why? Why should they learn it? How can I justify it, and what will my child understand? Ah-ha! Writing out checks, that's it.

The next time I go to the store (or I specifically go that day if necessary), I include my child in the check-writing process. I point out where I write the date, how I have to print the numbers as well as handwrite them, where I write the memo so I remember what the money was used for, and then show them how I sign with a flourish.

After I hand over the check, I show them where I record the check and do the math.

At that point, I've just introduced responsibility for money records, the fun in signing a name, and I made reference points to things they already know, like numbers and dates. It's done naturally, as a "hey, look at this, isn't it neat?" sort of way, with no mention of learning at all.

A few days later when we open the math book to handwritten numbers, they groan at the new, difficult looking stuff they have to learn. But I point out how they already "know" this, and I show them my checkbook to remind them of those handwritten numbers. I list the places I use checks, helping them understand why, applicably, learning to handwrite their numbers is necessary.

Here's an example of such a conversation:

"Oh, hey!" I exclaim, "This will be easy! You already know this!"

"Huh? Whaddya mean?" my son retorts gloomily, "I've never seen this before."

Ignoring his dark look of disgust, I fetch my purse, pull out my wallet, and show him and his sister the checkbook. "Look! Right here. Remember I had to write out the numbers as well as just print them?"

Oh. Yeah. Well, it doesn't mean they're convinced that they need to know it, though. Undaunted and prepared, I point out that they need to know how to spell out their numbers in order to write a check.

"I don't need to know that. I'm not gonna write any checks when I grow up!"

"Oh." I nod slowly and thoughtfully to give appropriate consideration. Then I have a question for him. "The DMV requires checks. So does this mean you probably won't own a car?"

"No, I'm gonna buy me a truck."

"You cannot pay for the license plate without a check. How will you do that?"

He thinks about it and finally concedes, "Alright, I'll learn it, but just so I can write my checks for the DMV."

That works for me. Instead of meaningless random numbers, I will speak money language as I work with him in writing his numbers. I will say, "two thousand, six hundred eighty-five dollars," not just the number 2,685. Just in case he needs a little extra persuasion, I show him how someone can alter the numerals on a check. Then I demonstrate how correctly handwritten numbers keep this type of forgery from happening. For their own sakes, they will now want to learn how to write out their numbers.

In fact, I may deviate from the book's practice problems at this point and make my own practice problems in the form of checks, asking them to find the checks that were not written properly. Like counterfeit money, one must know the right way in order to detect the wrong way. And now I've connected the learning of handwritten numbers to real life. They understand why they need to learn this.

For an added incentive, you can practice writing checks for a special treat or benefit. For example, write numbers on the whiteboard with the corresponding treat or benefit next to it. If they write out $8,327 properly, they have "bought" mom's assistance with a specific chore for that day. (Moms are *very* expensive for hire!) They get to sign their name in the flourish of their choice. It lends a sense of satisfaction, especially to the one who hates writing and is able to legitimately scribble his signature this time.

Truthfully, you could go through this whole scenario without ever cracking open a math book. They don't even have to associate this with "school" as much as, "Hey, you need to know this for when you start earning money and people pay you with checks." How do you know what they need to know? Pay attention to things you need to know and start from there. If I need or have needed to know something, then chances are high that they will, too.

When they're really young, lay stepping stones for what you'll be teaching them down the road. My kids learned about fractions through baking, long before they encountered them in their math book. Just keep it fun, keep it meaningful, and be aware of good timing. In this way, you can connect real life to each of the three R's and beyond.

WISDOM TO KNOW WHEN

It is important to know your child well enough to tailor your teaching style and timing. We all learn more quickly when we're enjoying what we are learning and we're ready to learn it.

• • • • • • • • • • •

It's usually a matter of when and how we learn that makes the biggest difference.

• • • • • • • • • • •

If you notice that your daughter likes figuring out how things work, go find old things for her to tinker around with and fix. Use that interest to guide her attention towards school. If your son shows an interest in cooking, let him help you and then introduce math through recipes. Pay attention to your child's interests and what they gravitate toward.

Once you know where your child's strengths and interests lie, start there for school. It is easier to start where they already hold an interest. Then you can integrate other areas of school into that place of interest. Concentrate and build on their God-given talents and interests. It will decrease the amount of frustration and discouragement you will feel from pressuring them where they have no interest or are not ready to go.

Choose your battles wisely. Math or any other subject is not a mountain to die on. Home life and school life are not separate. What happens in one area will certainly affect the other. Help your child win. Help them win battles of character instead of engaging them in battles over curriculum.

Mothers matter. Study your child, learn how she operates and what makes her tick. Teach her accordingly and watch her flourish under your care. Be her number one cheerleader and source of encouragement. As Edison later said, "My mother was the making of me. She was so true, so sure of me: and I felt I had something to live for, someone I must not disappoint."[3]

CHAPTER 6
OWN THE ATMOSPHERE

The bright morning sun is shining in through the windows. Fresh scents of lilac or lemon invigorate the air. A trio of candles flicker brightly on the countertop. Your favorite music is playing softly in the background. The room is warm and relaxing, yet inviting and refreshing. Who wouldn't want to join in?

The physical and emotional climate of your home affects the surrounding sense of peace and well-being for everyone present. There are some simple yet effective things that can help set the tone and atmosphere of your home to be a pleasant, calm, and stimulating learning environment.

SETTING THE TONE

I remember hearing a cheery "Good morning!" from my mom every morning, without fail. It was one of the things that greeted me, along with the smell of fried eggs and toast as I slid into my chair for breakfast. I also remember the aromas that often lingered in the air from baking bread or cookies, roasting pumpkin seeds, or the simmering of supper in a crockpot. Mom was usually in the kitchen working with food as she schooled us.

Setting the tone and atmosphere for the day can be quick and easy to do. You can do it with a couple of simple things. If you're not into a lot of baking, you can burn candles or use an oil diffuser with cinnamon, lemon, or the scent of your choice. Lemon is stimulating to the brain for learning. Candles add a calming effect. And soft background music can help the brain to focus and concentrate.

If you do bake, or will be preparing a crockpot for supper or doing some food prep, let the kids take breaks often and help you. Giving frequent breaks for outside exercise, to do a project, or working on some housework together gives their brain the needed rest periods from studying.

My parents had a dedicated "school room" with desks, bookshelves, a chalkboard, and art supplies. However, my siblings in their younger years did their homework at the kitchen table where Mom taught and supervised them as she worked.

As we became more independent in our studies, we transitioned to the schoolroom where it was quieter if we needed it. We took breaks a lot, and the change of scenery, sounds, and an occasional snack was energizing and revitalizing. Sometimes, we even took our schoolbooks outside to work on them.

• • • • • • • •

> Your home does not need to resemble a classroom in order for your children to learn.

• • • • • • • •

It is first and foremost a home where they are learning life skills, of which curriculum plays a part. We had no extra room to dedicate for a schoolroom for my own children, so we used the kitchen table. If you like the idea of a dedicated schoolroom, that's great, but it's also not necessary.

ROUTINE/FLEXIBILITY PARADOX

Children thrive on consistency. They gain comfort and security from regularity in their lives, and they flourish when they know what is expected of them. Having things that remain routine each day is healthy and helpful to the homeschool experience. These constants need to be within your control. What you can do every day.

Be prepared to meet those things outside of your control with a smile. Learn to be flexible, and make adjustments as needed. No day will go perfectly as planned—that's something you can plan on. It's how you respond to the interruptions, delays, or disturbances that make a bigger difference than the interferences themselves. Have a flexible routine and a routine flexibility.

Establish consistency and order, with time and attitude built in, to allow for the flow of life. This provides your children with an environment to thrive in and supports their mental and emotional state of mind, which in turn affects their ability to learn and retain.

LOOK FOR OPEN DOORS

Let's say your daily schedule after lunch is to read a story before an hour of quiet/nap time. During lunch cleanup, your big helper rearranges some items in order to put leftovers back in the fridge. As she does so, she drops a carton of eggs. You needed those eggs for baking a jelly roll that afternoon and for the quiche you've planned for supper. Now what?

One response is frustration at the delay in schedule, irritation at your child for not being more careful, and annoyance at the need for a special grocery trip. Though all these things may be true, those reactions will not repair a derailed day. How can you use an incident like this to your advantage? How can you show what is important in life, create a teachable moment, and fuel an interest in learning?

You clean up the mess with your big helper, showing her how to do it without making a bigger mess. As you do so, you notice that one egg remains uncracked. You decide it is now of more use for an educational moment since you'll be needing more than one egg for your baking. You say "Hey! Did you know…?" and share with her that an egg cannot be broken when it's squeezed from end to end.

Of course, with all the broken eggs you're in the midst of cleaning up, she sees the fragility of eggs and doesn't believe you. "Give it a try," you encourage. "You won't make a bigger mess than the one we're cleaning up already." Well, that's an unexpected and tempting offer. You show her how to hold it, and she squeezes with all her might, even using both hands, but cannot break the egg.

Her brother standing by is sure that he can do it and also gives it a try, but without success. "How can eggs break so easily, yet be so hard to break?" Now they are super curious, and you tell them you'll find a book to learn more about it later.

After story time and putting them down for quiet time and naps, you reroute your afternoon … either change the baking day and supper menu, or swap afternoon agendas in order to run to the store after the children are up from their naps. You have effectively kept to the stabilizing routine of story time and quiet time yet remained adaptable to the afternoon's changes.

As a bonus, you also have an open door with your child to willingly enter the world of science and physics. First, you'll learn how the shape of an egg helps to distribute forces across its surface of up to a whopping ninety pounds. From there, you can branch into all sorts of fun things, like learning how to get an egg to stand on end, how to crack an egg with one hand, why a hard-boiled egg spins differently than a raw egg, and why airplane engineers study the egg's shape and resistance to shattering.

• • • • • • • • • •

All of this is possible when you are on the lookout for teachable moments.

• • • • • • • • • •

When you take what could be a negative moment and turn it into a learning one, the example above could go on and on. Shifting from airplane engineers and how airplanes fly, to weather and the types of clouds, to the sun and its effects on the earth, to the layers of earth and learning what dirt is made out of, to the kinds of rocks and a rock collection, to plants and growing indoor seedlings for the garden. The list is endless.

INTRODUCE A TOPIC NATURALLY

One such example of an open door is a door into math through counting money. Think about how you can introduce counting money as naturally as possible as you go about your day.

In a way that keeps your child busy, plus gets something accomplished, have them do little odd jobs like swatting flies, dead-heading dandelions, removing sticks out of the yard or rocks out of the garden. Offer the motivation of money. Give a penny, nickel, dime, or quarter each, depending on the job, their age and understanding, and your pocketbook.

Then, have them save their money in a piggy bank. As the change grows, count it with them. Show them how to count the coins they've earned. If you normally offer pennies and an occasional nickel, be purposeful to give at least one bigger job each for a dime and a quarter. This way, they'll have all the coins to count.

You can show them how just *one* quarter is equal to *twenty-five* pennies or *five* nickels, and so on. Once their stash reaches a certain amount (at least $1.10 to allow for tax), have them bring it with them on your next trip to town and take it to a coin counter to exchange for bill(s). Your local bank, grocery store, or pharmacy will often have a coin counter inside.

The kids may feel a bit discouraged at first to see all that change equal so little. Be sure to prep them that holding a *whole* dollar bill is like having *a hundred* pennies! They will eventually understand the conversion value and get super excited about the number of dollar bills they receive.

Next, take them to a dollar store. Before you go in, give them a brief explanation about taxes. Keep it simple and positive. They don't need the burden of tax on their shoulders yet, just a simple concept of it. You can educate them further and share your opinions on taxation at a later date. But teaching them the concept of tax dispels the idea that the price shown is their final expense.

"Honey, everything in this store is $1.00, but in addition to paying $1.00, you will need to pay tax. Tax is a little extra money we pay to the government on everything we buy. The money goes to help pay for a lot of different things, like our roads, our parks, the military, and to help people who have disabilities."

Take them into the store and let them pick out whatever they want (within your guidelines, of course). Then have them pay for it with the money they just exchanged. They will love this. They will also be motivated to continue doing more odd jobs to earn money.

This is an excellent way to encourage a work ethic: to have them earn money for their own desired expenditures, to learn money management and how to spend wisely, and to develop an appreciation for what they buy. As they get older, they may choose to buy immediately at the minimum savings required or save for a larger spending trip or desired item.

As they get older, you can challenge their counting skills by timing them. Count a pile of coins correctly in so many seconds. Count by stacking the coins in nickels, dimes, and quarters to equal a dollar. We would offer a coin reward or special privilege when they could finish counting before the timer went off.

We'd decrease the timer and increase the reward as they got older. Our 9- and 12-year-olds would still be challenged by stacking coins into dollar piles, and they loved earning money and privileges this way. Sometimes it was a fun contest between parent and child. They got to be really quick and accurate. (You can compete against your younger children, too. Just give yourself waaaaay more coins to count.)

AVOIDING OVERLOAD AND OVERWHELM

Another area that can shift the atmosphere in our home is how well we manage our daily load. The last thing any of us are good at is creativity and consistency when we're worn thin, exhausted, overloaded, and overwhelmed. We're far more likely to drop the ball, let things slide, or begin to nag or nitpick at the slightest thing.

● ● ● ● ● ● ● ● ● ●

In addition to having a flexible schedule, have reasonable expectations as well.

● ● ● ● ● ● ● ● ● ●

What can we reasonably expect to get done in a day? We need to be real with ourselves and our calendar. For everything we say "yes" to, it usually requires saying "no" to at least one or two other things. The problem is when we don't consciously realize this. Later, we run ourselves crazy trying to juggle everything.

I used to be a master at juggling. I was proud of my multitasking skills. I could beat everyone in my family, hands down. However, it was only a matter of time before I learned a non-negotiable truth about life. We all have limits. When those limits are reached, chaos and instability take over. I now struggle to juggle more than a couple of things. And I openly acknowledge my lack for effective multitasking.

I am still a very able and capable person. I just learned the limits of any human being. We may be able to juggle a couple things well for a longer period of time. We may be able to juggle many things for a shorter period of time. But no one can juggle many things over a long period without eventually having a fallout or burnout.

I have learned that it is possible to avoid the painful consequences if we properly manage the amount we can juggle or manage on a long-term basis. One item in means one item out. Accepting a heavier weighted or time-consuming item may mean eliminating three other items to make room. The equivalent of its burden must be removed. We have a certain capacity and, once filled, we ride the danger zone if we do not make the necessary adjustments.

Needless to say, we take our children on the roller coaster ride with us. They quickly pick up and reflect the tone and temperature of their surroundings. When we are able to be relaxed and confident, they will be, too. But when we have overloaded ourselves, taking on more than we can possibly sustain, they also pay a price.

So how do we decide what to keep and what to remove? First identify your priorities. Write them down and post them where you'll see them often, as a reminder for your ongoing daily decisions. One of my favorite places is in the bathroom. Every time I use the toilet, I am reminded of my priorities. As everyone else in the household also sees my notes, it also makes for compelling accountability.

Next, ask yourself some questions. What things are necessary and relevant to your priorities? What things can be eliminated? What can be automated? And what can be delegated? Remember, there is only one of you. And there is only so much you can do. When you decrease your load to reasonable, you will feel yourself relax, and everything will look a lot more doable.

Being responsible for yourself will help your children learn how to be responsible for themselves. When they see you taking on too much, they will either follow suit and become overly responsible and stressed out, or they will take advantage of your over-responsible nature and become irresponsible themselves.

It is healthy to learn the difference between being responsible *to* and responsible *for*, and to know when you're *not* responsible. Having good boundaries and demonstrating them is a powerful strength and tool in your toolbox.

CHAPTER 7
HOW TO CREATE INTEREST FOR LEARNING

Learning is not some horrible, dreaded disease. Learning is a gift. Learning is a privilege. Learning gives us freedom. Learning is exhilarating and satisfying. It provides accomplishment and achievement. It brings fulfillment and rest. We were created with a natural curiosity to question, learn, create, and problem solve.

● ● ● ● ● ● ● ● ● ●

Learning is Living, Enjoying, Asking, Recognizing, and Noticing.

● ● ● ● ● ● ● ● ● ●

CREATED TO ENJOY LEARNING

Babies are interested in everything around them. How it tastes, how it feels, how it sounds, how it looks, and how it smells. Toddlers are also interested in learning. How it works, how it breaks, how it goes back together (if it goes back together!), what it is made out of, how long it will get, what will fit into where, and so on. The list is nearly endless for a toddler, as you know. They want to know the why and how for everything.

So, when does this natural curiosity end? What puts out the fire of their interest? How do they go from curious about everything to disinterested and detached from learning? What puts a damper on it?

The answers:

> When it is no longer fun.
>
> When we begin to apply pressure to learn.
>
> When we sit them down at a table or desk for long periods of boring "learning."
>
> When the fun is taken away, the interest goes with it.

• • • • • • •

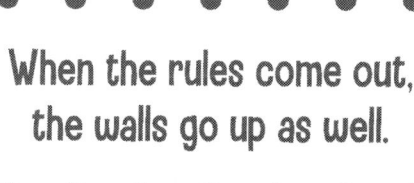

• • • • • • •

What then? How can we break down that wall of indifference to learning? Left to themselves, children often put the brakes on and rebel when anyone tries to tell them what to do. They have a natural tendency to refuse instruction and do exactly as they were told not to. So how do we cultivate and rekindle an interest in learning?

ASK QUESTIONS!

We ask questions. Lots of questions. Think about how many times you asked your baby toddler questions as he was simply playing. What is that? Where does it go? What do you see? How many are there? What color is it?

When you had your toddler on your lap and were trying to help him put a shape in the right spot, how well did it go when you told him where to put it? Or did he grunt and try a different place, or several other places, first? How often did he just let you tell him where to place it and how often did he want to figure it out for himself? How quickly did you get wise to the fact that he responded better when you asked him questions to lead him to the answer? "Where does it go? Which one has a point on it like this one?"

Questions stimulate the brain. When asked a question, our brain seeks to find an answer. It starts the thinking process. Questions open up possibilities and get our creative juices flowing. Questions capture our attention. One question can have us pondering for hours.

On the other hand, when we're told a statement, we do not have to think. We most often react. We react either positively and accept what we're being told, or negatively and reject what we're being told. If we've already decided we want to hear what another person has to say, or we like them, we'll be likely to accept what they're saying. But if not, we are quick to dismiss or reject their words and forget about them.

As we approach our child for school, we need to harness the power of questions and use that power of curiosity to our advantage. We must also do it first in the context of life, if we want them to remain open and interested. Schooling found in books before it is encountered in life is meaningless.

INVEST EARLY

Start young. Allow your children to engage in meaningful things, even when their "help" is not really helpful. This encourages them to participate and instills a love for learning new things. Enlist their help and let them assist you, even when you could have done it better, quicker, more easily without them. You are investing into their lives. One day, they will be the ones outperforming you.

Invite their assistance whenever, wherever, and however you can. It doesn't matter how small or insignificant it may seem, never allow them to simply be a spectator. Involve them in your daily life. Letting them "help" when they are too young to know better sets the stage for their becoming your best helper as they get older.

Let them help you sweep by picking things up or holding the dustpan for you, then manning the sweeper itself when they can do so. Have them start by rinsing the dishes, then by helping you wash them. Let them help pour and add ingredients, then crack eggs and operate the blender. Let them drop seeds into the ground, then allow them to water. Let them help harvest by putting the produce into a bucket, then aid in picking. Have them hand you

HOW TO CREATE INTEREST FOR LEARNING

the nails and hammer, then progress to holding down boards and helping you measure.

But don't isolate this pattern of assistance to your home. Your children will get extra excited to be helping out in a public place. They feel quite grown up getting to do things they see other adults doing.

If you are grocery shopping with your one-year-old, let them hold an item for you. Let your two-year-old take items from you to place in the cart. Let your three or four-year-old pick up items from the shelf and hand them to the two-year-old. They will learn how to follow directions and relate to each other under your supervision.

Having them help you in the grocery store when they are very young leads to their cooperation in the grocery buying process. You show them how to check for the freshness date. You demonstrate how to pick out good produce. You show them about price per ounce and have them help you find the best deal.

Later, you will be able to send them down a separate aisle because they know just what to look for. You will also be able to connect their experiences to their schoolwork. You can associate money and the decimal point, leading into math problems involving price per unit. It will make sense to them since they first encountered it in life, and they know why they need to understand it.

Doing this will give you a wide-open door to introduce all sorts of topics and interests into their lives. And it will give you an opportunity to understand your child's interests better. You'll learn their preferences, inclinations, and aptitudes. Then, you can build off what you have learned so you can individualize your approach with them for school.

SHOW AND TELL

Allowing and inviting your children into your world stimulates their curiosity. God created your child to emulate you. If you demonstrate a fascination and excitement to learn, know, and understand, you will spark their interest and they will follow suit.

While they were young toddlers, I would talk with my children as I did things and went places. I would show them things and "inform" them on topics that they could not yet fully understand. Sometimes they had no idea what I was talking about. However, what they did catch was that I was including them into my life. As I made a habit of doing this, it would amaze me how much they actually started picking up on things. Then they would ask questions that gave me an opportunity to share more information with them. I would explain the best I could, knowing that as they got older, they would continue to grasp more each time I talked about it: line upon line and here a little, there a little, in practice.

It was from this place of fellowship that I did a lot of early teaching. Your child needs to be in relationship with you first and foremost. It is within the context of relationship that schooling is most effective.

BE INTENTIONAL

When I wanted to share something with my child, I would approach it with intentional excitement. If I was going to interest them in helping me, I needed to make it sound and look as exciting as possible. It usually worked, just like when you tempt a baby to crawl over to you. You have to give incentives and make something look interesting enough to pique their interest. It's really no different as your child matures. You just have to make it age-appropriate, all the way through their teens.

> **Knowing what your child likes and then hooking their interest with a question works like a charm every time.**

This strategy employs how our brains were created to respond. We are not terribly interested in something completely new that we cannot relate to. However, if you can link it to what they already hold an interest in, or something that directly affects them, you've got yourself a catch.

Always be on the lookout for opportunities to point out something. Be intentional about topics and give forethought as to how you frame your questions. You want to ask questions to get them thinking. Even if it is only for a couple minutes, take the time to consider where you want to direct their attention. Use questions that pertain to their life settings and surroundings. Then use more questions, thinking aloud, wondering, and silly theories to engage and raise their interest.

"Thinking" out loud is another wonderful tool to stimulate their brains and interactions with you. The educational term is "metacognition" and is a proven strategy that helps students understand what you are thinking so they can learn what they are thinking, how they are thinking about it, and why. It is a powerful tool. You can "wonder" about so many things. And it gets them wondering, too. Then, curiosity begins to take root. When cultivated and watered, it grows into an area of interest and they want to find out more (i.e., *learn!*).

I WONDER AS I WANDER

A great place to think aloud and wonder is while driving. As I drove, I often commented on the weather. Weather affects a child tremendously. For one thing, it determines whether or not he'll be able to go outside to play. Veering from the direct topic of the weather, I would branch out into all sorts of other science topics, leading them towards something I wanted to gain their interest in.

"Wow, isn't it a beautiful day? Look at the clouds! I think that cloud looks like an elephant. Oh, you think that one looks like an ice cream cone? Wouldn't that be fun to sit on a cloud and eat ice cream? I wonder if we'd be able to sit on the clouds or if we'd fall right through. You think it would hold us? Now look at those clouds over there. They look different. Like they got pulled apart. I don't think we could sit on those clouds. I wonder what makes the difference between the clouds…"

Contemplating clouds leads to learning how they are different. This then opens up the conversation to weather and atmosphere. Pointing out shapes leads to geometry. Colors lead to primary colors and color blends. Letters lead to sounds and reading, of course. And numbers lead to math.

I found that by introducing topics through nature and outdoor life, I could bring the concepts indoors to study them. And I discovered that the habit of discussing things while driving offered me the benefit of an endless variety of subjects in an ever-changing environment.

LEARNING IS FUN - KEEP IT THAT WAY

Adding humor to the learning process in everyday life paves the way to conversations, participation, and interest. Here is an example of using questions, thinking out loud, wondering, and gaining my children's attention. In this case, I desired to introduce the concept of chlorophyll while driving to the grocery store.

"Oooh, look at that!" I exclaimed over the beauty of the budding trees passing by. I began to wonder how they got that way. I talked about the bright green grass and the budding trees in the spring and wondered how the leaves turned green.

"They just turn green," a child states pragmatically.

"Yes, but how?" I respond, puzzled. "Do you think there is green ink inside the tree? Like a big green marker coloring all the leaves green?"

"NO!" they laugh. But the super-silly comment gets them more interested in the conversation. Next I present a theory.

"Maybe it's the rain that makes them turn green. Maybe at night when we can't see it, the rain turns green and it paints the grass and leaves." I am all serious. They study my face, doubtful.

"Let's check the grass when we get out and see if it's paint. I want to see if I can rub it off." They remain uncertain but agree to help me look. When we arrive, they pile out of the van, and I stoop to pull a blade of grass to examine it.

"Nope. It's not paint," I confirm. "It doesn't come off. Hmmm. That's interesting."

As we walk into the store, the question lingers on their minds. As we go down the aisles, they start offering up their own suggestions and ideas. This is exactly what I wanted. Their little minds are percolating. I don't shoot down any wild ideas, I just ask more questions. Sometimes a theory ends way out in left field. No matter.

In a light-bulb moment, I offer, "Hey, why don't we stop at the library on our way home and see if they have a book that can tell us how the leaves and grass turn green?"

"Yes!" they agree emphatically. Now they have a need to know for themselves. We make a quick stop by the library and they page through the book on our way home, using the pictures to make further guesses.

As soon as we put away our groceries, we sit down, and I read them the book. We all ooh and ahh at the explanation about chlorophyll, and then laugh and rib each other about how wrong we were with our guesses. I usually got laughed at the most, seeing as I was the mom and should have known better. Yep, but I'll never tell.

HOW TO CREATE INTEREST FOR LEARNING

Over supper that night, chlorophyll is the topic at the dinner table. The kids stumble over themselves to share with Dad what they just learned. They take great delight in the re-telling of Mom's failed theory.

Stories like these made it into our family archives. "Hey, remember when…," followed with gales of laughter. My oldest son in particular loved to try to best me in my theories. As he got older and I would hypothesize about something I knew nothing about, it was great fun to learn about something together.

Learning should be fun and spark creativity. Your goal is to keep it that way. Kids gravitate towards fun, happy, and exciting.

Remember that even after they've learned something, you don't have to connect it immediately to school. It's later when you introduce a topic in school that you refer back to what they had already learned and know. This diminishes the fear of something new.

Please be careful that as you teach your child, you do not become a bully. The less time they have to sit trapped behind a table or desk, the better. And the more quickly they can complete their necessary paperwork, the happier they'll be.

CHAPTER 8
WONDERS OF THE WHITEBOARD

The whiteboard became and has remained one of the most effective and efficient tools in my house for both home life and school. It has become worth more than its weight in gold to me. These boards hold some central places on my walls. They have served me well from teaching my youngsters to read, to helping maintain order and peace in the home, to communicating with my older teens, and everything in between. In fact, my daughter and I used a whiteboard in the organizing of this book.

MY FAVORITE SCHOOL TOOL

I first discovered the wonders of the whiteboard while living in South Korea. We lived in a tiny old brick house where we had very little room for what would be considered necessities in the States. I experienced the truth about necessity being the mother of invention.

Since we ate on the floor, I had no table at which to teach the children. We nearly needed stop lights for the one-way traffic allowable in most of our space. Our queen bed was the largest flat area in our home. Since the internet cable brought in through the bedroom window already placed the computer in our bedroom, I decided to utilize the room as our schoolroom as well.

Instead of the usual picture above the bed, I hung a large whiteboard. I sectioned the white space to hold our weekly calendar, prayer requests, reminders, and a to-do list. I also used it to teach school. I bought the children smaller personal whiteboards to practice with and use in lieu of the scrap paper we didn't have.

I quickly began to learn about the advantages of a whiteboard as an all-purpose house and school tool. I also learned that it made a great tool for family communication and clarification. I got a couple more whiteboards of different sizes to hang in the kitchen for grocery lists and in the kids' bedroom for chore lists.

AN EFFECTIVE "WEAPON"

During my earlier homeschool years, when I got stumped in math my dad would go to the chalkboard to explain and demonstrate. From learning long division to having trouble with metric system conversion, I caught on to things better at the chalkboard. There is a reason for this.

Our brains notice and recall certain things more easily than others. Regarding memory, bigger is better. We take note of things that are excessive, huge, outlandish, and out of proportion, both in size and number. We remember things that are colorful, silly, crazy, and out of the ordinary. Painful things also catch our attention, with imaginations that make us shiver, shudder, and grimace.

In application, what this means is that the larger-than-type letters, numbers, and pictures drawn on a chalkboard or whiteboard make it easier for the brain to make sense of, process, and recall the information. This is why children's beginner books use larger type. Once they become proficient in reading, they are able to read the smaller type without a problem.

Thus, having a larger board to see things on and being able to practice in larger handwriting helps the child's brain to learn and remember. There's also just something about the easy "erase-ableness" of a chalkboard or whiteboard that is less intimidating than using a pencil and eraser on paper. One swipe, and a mistake can easily be corrected. It makes for great teaching and practice.

POWER OF ILLUSTRATION

Illustrating with the whiteboard is remarkably effective, especially when done in a memorable way by utilizing the exaggerations that our brains take notice of.

• • • • • • • • •

The possibilities that arise using a combination effect for multiple learning preferences is impressive.

• • • • • • • • •

The picture- and word-oriented brains are activated as they see the drawings in progress and see the bigger-than-print written words. The logic-oriented brains are stimulated as they hear the explanations. The music-oriented brains are triggered when you incorporate a song or rhythm into your demonstrations.

You can include the movement-oriented student by having them participate with their own whiteboard or put actions to what you are drawing on the board. The awesome thing is that most of us have a combination of learning preferences, so usually one of these styles will hit a sweet spot.

For example, I draw a quick outline of the United States as I illustrate a point regarding geography. I laugh as I notice that my outline more resembles a giant elongated tooth. The kids might snicker at it, but they'll remember a reference to "the drawing that looked like a tooth." The connection between a tooth and a country is far-fetched and unlikely…thus easier to remember, actually. It's the normal and common that are more difficult to recall.

As I make my illustration, I use big sweeping movements and add an element of silliness, both in what I say and how I say it. I may tap the marker repeatedly in the Atlantic Ocean as I repeat in a sing-songy voice, or a rhythmic tone, "*Eeeeeeeeeast*! On the *Eeeeeeeast* Coast."

For an added earth science demonstration, I might draw a high-arching dotted line with a big arrow to the west coast to show the direction the sun moves. They'll be more likely to remember the information I am illustrating when I emphasize and connect it with humor, drama, and over-exaggeration.

For a predominantly movement-oriented learner, tweak the above example by having them draw their own illustration along with you, or have them be the main demonstrator for a younger sibling. You can still incorporate some of the other learning styles: "Let's draw the U.S. It looks something like this. Now, where is the East Coast? The *e, e, e, e, Eeeeeast* Coast? Good! Now let's draw a line towards the west..." Do this while demonstrating sweeping arm movements as they draw.

If I were to illustrate a math point, I would give my child practice problems on the board before going to the textbook. That way, like reading large text, the printed math problems will not seem as hard after practicing with larger diagrams. If they still struggle, I have them solve the problems on their individual whiteboard, then with a blank sheet of paper, until they are comfortable with the smaller print in their books.

LEARNING TO READ

While in South Korea, I wrote out large cards of common words and posted them all around our tiny house: wall, floor, ceiling, table, chair, toaster, dresser, mirror, bed, washer, sink, oven, counter, computer, toilet, etc. I'd point to them as I said the word and referred to it. They began to learn these words by sight.

When my two youngest began asking to learn to read, I gave them letter cards to practice sounding out. I put consonants and vowels together, such as *ba, be, bi, bo, bu*. Once they knew how each of the consonants blended with the five vowels, I would write consonant-vowel blends on the whiteboard for them to recognize and say out loud.

I made a game of it. I wrote several blends on the board. I'd point to a blend. As they gave the correct sound, I'd erase it. The rule was that I had to set down the eraser each time after erasing a blend. It wasn't long before they got quicker at saying the blends than I could erase. From there, I moved on to three-letter words.

The first time I wrote out a three-letter word, my son asked, "Mom, what's that? It's got an extra letter at the end."

"This is a word." I replied. I covered the last letter of the word *bat* that I'd written and asked, "What's this?" They immediately answered, *ba*. Then I uncovered the last letter. "Now add this sound to the end," I said.

"Ba–t…ba–t…bat!" Yes! My son was excited. I erased the *t* and added a *g*. Ba–g…bag! "You're getting it! Now this one." I erased the *b* and replaced it with an *r*. After a moment, the answer came, "Rag!" I continued leading them along by changing one letter at a time. From rag to rat to sat to sit to fit to fig to big to beg to egg to hog to hug to rug. They were so excited. They could read!

That very night they were deep into the few books we had on hand, trying to find words that they knew and pointing them out. The next day I taught them about blends. End blends like cold, bark, next, and mist. Beginning blends like skin, spot, glad, and from. Blends on both ends like stand, blast, trunk, and drift. And middle letters and blends like kitten, muffin, mister, and alter. I did this all on the whiteboard, where I could write in larger-than-life letters and use different colors.

We progressed with the various vowel blends like *oi* and *oy*, *au* and *aw*. Then came the long vowel words and the rule of silent *e* for name and cone. From there, we went through other rules and exceptions. *Y* for baby and cry. The silent *b* in climb and thumb. The silent *gh* in night and through. The *d* and *t* for past tenses.

By now they were nearly reading whole small books. They'd come to me for a word they didn't know and I'd explain a new rule or exception, or refer them to one of the rules we'd already learned. As they came with questions, all I had to do was answer and they were quick to apply what I said to even more new words. Their vocabulary grew swiftly.

My children became bookworms. I found a library a half hour away where we could check out English books. Each week they maxed out their limit of ten books. They read and reread the books over and over, growing in their vocabulary and reading skills.

READING PREP

To be sure, we did not magically end up at this whiteboard moment. Plenty of reading prep took place long before the crowning glory of a successful reading launch occurred.

Reading aloud to your children when they are younger helps their reading and comprehension skills when they are older. It also helps them gain respect and a healthy interest for books.

I would sing nursery rhyme books to my children when they were babies and toddlers. We always had "book time" before going down for a nap and in our bedtime routine. I also read many other types of books to them as they got older.

Find your child's interest and follow it.

At two years old, my oldest son was so interested in airplanes that I looked for an airplane magazine. There were no children magazines available, so I ordered an adult magazine, *Private Pilot*. When it arrived, I was a bit skeptical about it, since there weren't as many pictures in it as I'd hoped for.

However, my son would sit for lengths of time looking through the magazine. When he'd ask me to read it to him, I figured he'd get bored after some time, while I read pages without pictures. Not so. I couldn't believe his attention span while I read things I didn't even understand.

Reading what your child is interested in will help pique their interest in books. It will bring them to a point of desiring to read and asking to learn to read.

READING BASICS

I began preparing my children for reading from the time they were toddlers. I'd make silly letter sounds, sing, play, associate letters to sounds, and play games-on-the-go while driving. I wanted to lay an early foundation so that when they were ready, they would be prepared to ease into the final steps of constructing the sounds into words.

Along with the nursery rhymes and other such baby books, I read and sang books about the ABCs, numbers, shapes, colors, animals, etc., to my infant and toddler children. I usually invested an hour or more in books every day. I wanted to whet my children's appetite for books and have them experience the pleasure of discovering what lay between the book covers.

While reading an ABC book, I'd emphasize each letter sound for the word and then relate it to them in some way, often in question form. "*A* is for apple...*a-a-apple*. Yummy apple, we just had apples for lunch, didn't we? *B* is for ball...*b-b-ball*. What color is your ball? *C* is for cat...*c-c-cat*. Our cat is Oreo. Where is Oreo?"

I built on these letter sounds in the number book whenever I could. "*T...t-t-two*. Two carrots. Carrots starts with a *c...c-c-carrot*." It didn't matter that they didn't immediately understand. Their little brains were soaking it up, becoming familiar with patterns and sounds. This is what I used to build on.

As I read or sang through other books, I'd have conversations that began one-sided. "Ooooh, look! What's this? *F* is for *frog*. It's green and has big eyes and long, jumping legs. It's a frog! *F-f-frog*! How does a frog go? *Rrrrrrr-ribbet, rrrrrrr-ribbet*!" As I say "ribbet," I gently bounce them on my knee, mimicking a jumping frog. (Notice, I am gaining their attention, including movement, giving information, and emphasizing sounds for them.)

When the child got old enough to respond, I continued to give him more information and kept asking questions, keeping it exciting and fun. "Ah-ha! What do we have here? Yes! *H* is for horse. *H-h-horse*. But what is he going to do? Where is he going to go? Let's keep reading to find out!" After turning the page, "Oh my, look at this!

What a mess! He should go over to the pond and get cleaned off, shouldn't he? Look over here by the water—how does this frog go? That's right! Maybe the frog is saying, *Rrrrrrr-ribbet*, take a bath! *R* is for *rrrrrr-ribbet, rrrrrrr-ribbet!*" Again, I bounce when I ribbet. (I'm reinforcing previous information and building on it.)

Once I captured their attention and they loved the storybook, I began to more purposely target the alphabet letters. "There goes that silly horse into the mud again! What does the word 'horse' start with? Good job! And how does the frog go? That's right—*rrrrrrr-ribbet!* What does 'ribbet' start with? An *r*, yes!"

My oldest and youngest children were more interactive and responsive than my middle son was. I didn't make a big deal of it when he didn't answer a question. I paused, gave him a chance to respond, then answered my own question and went on. The last thing I wanted to do was create pressure while trying to make reading a book fun. He was still listening and absorbing, so there was no need to push.

BUILDING ON THE BASICS

In addition to the reading, I would sing the ABC song while making a meal, driving in the van, or out for a walk. I sang each letter with clear enunciation so that *l-m-n-o-p* did not become an unrecognizable mess to my child by singing it too fast. I'd also sing the little songs from books like *The Wheels on the Bus*.

As we'd sing, sometimes I'd interrupt the song with questions like, "How many wheels are on the bus?—Four! *One, t-two, thr-thr-three, f-f-f-four!*" (emphasizing while counting on my fingers.) "Red and yellow, black and ___?—White! *W-white*. Just like *w-wet* and *w-window* and *w-wobbly*—a wet, wobbly window!" (with a laugh) "…*l-m-n-o-p*…what begins with *p*? *P-paint, p-pig, p-pull*. I *p*ull a *p*ig through *p*aint!" Make it fun and silly and they'll love singing and playing along with you.

I pointed out letters at home, on the road, and in books. I started by pointing out the first letter of a word. I began with words that were significant to them, like the first letter of their name, their pet's name, their favorite colors, a food they loved, etc. Whatever their interest, use it! "There's a *J* for James. *J-J-James*." "Look!—there's a *b* for *b-b-banana*." The goal is to connect a sound they are familiar with to its corresponding letter. I pointed out letters at home, on the road, and in books.

Now as I would read, I would follow along the words with my finger, stopping to point out letters they had begun to recognize. It wasn't long before they wanted to do the finger-following, so I showed them how to point to each word, left to right, top to bottom, in a slow, smooth fashion. They began to pick up the rhythm of reading, learning that a grouping of letters was a word, and that I had to finish reading one word before we could go on to the next one.

Before long, of course, they wanted to follow along by themselves, and it became a fun time of their dictating how slowly or quickly I read based off the pace that their finger was moving. I added fun inflections to reflect their finger speed. "The… wheels on the bus go rooooooouuuuunnnnnd aaaaaannnd rooooooouuuuunnnnnd, roundandround, roooouuunnnd and round!" Not only did we have a lot of laughs, this increased their participation into the reading process by their interaction with the printed words.

I was always on the lookout for opportunities to point out fresh letters. Whether it was on the flour bag while baking, their clothing tag, a road sign, or while grocery shopping. It became a natural progression for them to begin to spot letters and proudly point them out to me.

The word games followed us to church. While the Bible was being read, I would help my daughter follow along with her finger. She would be on the lookout for letters she recognized. During the sermon, she'd scour the page and point out letters she knew. Or I'd show her a certain letter and have her find more of them on the page. This is more difficult than it sounds because she was searching in tiny print, not the nice big letters of children's books, so this felt like quite an accomplishment to her.

ADVANCING IN THE BASICS

The next logical step is to introduce working with the letters. As my child became familiar with the letters and began to recognize them by name, I would begin to draw the letter in different ways and on different textures. Not immediately on paper, though.

Practicing with the ABC book, I'd trace his finger over the large *J* as I said, "*J* for James," letting him get the feel of how his finger and wrist moved. We used a stick to draw in the dirt, driveway or sandbox. A fogged-up mirror or window is always fun, too, of course.

From my therapy background, I knew that gross motor movement precedes fine motor movement. In other words, larger movements with the whole hand and wrist come before smaller movements with the fingers, like writing with a pencil. I found food play to be an effective place to start.

I would create letters (and shapes) out of as many food items as possible, pointing out colors, textures, fun facts, and adding to their vocabulary. Kids always eat, and what better way to reinforce learning than with their food? I'd look for foods to match a letter or make into letters. A pancake in the shape of a *J*. A pretzel stick in the form of an *l*. Pointing out the *o* of Cheerios, then biting them into a *c*. Making an *a* with a Cheerio and a short pretzel stick.

I always cut our sandwiches up into squares and triangles. Then we'd have a lot of fun eating them in a way that created a letter or another shape. Together we made edible playdough to form letters, decorate, and then eat them. We often arranged snack pieces like raisins into the shapes of letters, numbers, and shapes before eating them; and formed letters with cooked spaghetti was always entertaining. If something is going to get messy, just lay plastic wrap down beforehand for easy cleanup.

Fridge magnets are a wonderful tool. First for color recognition, then for numbers and letters and, eventually, for word building. Using plastic letters and playdough is a great combination.

Once your child gains full recognition of a letter or group of letters, it's time to pull out the finger paint or similar substance. Introduce your child to finger fun by painting letters onto paper. If they are motivated by eating, you can use something like thin frosting or chocolate syrup instead of finger paint.

BEYOND THE BASICS

It will only be a matter of time before your child will be recognizing enough letters to begin combining them into words. Be aware of letters you want to be sure to introduce into their vocabulary early on, especially their name letters.

If his name is Byron, you will need to find a way of making *y* significant to him. Read a book about yaks or zero in on a yarn picture. When he's tired, yawn with him, and point out that "yawn starts with a *y…y-y-yawn.*" (You can do this with any kind of action, which is helpful for the kinesthetic learner.) Highlight the color yellow and do the same. Point out the yellow sun, the yellow lemon and banana, the yellow daffodil, the yellow on the bees. Make each letter in his name significant like this to his world.

Once he is able to recognize all the letters to his name, start the process of putting those letters in order for him. Arrange the fridge magnets as you sound out his name. Form his name with snacks, noodles, playdough. Then write his name with fingerpaint. Say each letter and sound out his name as you write it. "*B…b-b-B. Y… Byyyyy. R…Byrrrrr. O…Byrooooo. N…Byronnnnnn.* Byron!"

If there is a silent letter, like I had with James, I simply told him, "This *e* doesn't make any sound in your name. It likes to stay quiet and hide. But we know it's there!" For the *s* I told him, "In your name, the *s* sounds like a *z*. Isn't that pretty cool?" They don't need to know all the phonetic rules for their name yet. Just the significance to them. A neat way to do this is to cut out pictures of what each letter stands for and glue them on a paper above their letters. For the "Byron" example: basketball, yogurt, rocket, Oscar (the Grouch), and Nerf ball.

After they demonstrated word recognition for their name, I pointed out other words, especially during book time. I chose a couple words that were meaningful to them and worked with them until they could easily pick them out. For instance, "car." I would point out "car" each time I read it in the car book. Emphasize the letter sounds, I said, "car...*c-c-caaaarrrr,*" pointing to each letter as I pronounced it. Then pointing to the word as a whole, I repeated, "C-a-r makes 'car'!" As we went through the book, I pointed my finger to each "car" word as I read, stopping at all of them.

I watched for places to reinforce the word. When we left to go somewhere, I'd say, "Let's go out to the car...the c-a-r!" Once we were on the road, I'd say something like, "Let's look for a red car." When we found one, I'd repeat, "A red car...*c-c-caaarrrr*...how do we spell car?" "C-a-r!" This is strengthening the correlation between the letters, the object, and the word, getting them familiar with how letters connect to create meaningful words.

One of the words I introduced was *the*. Since *the* does not follow the phonetic rules, I wanted them to recognize it by sight. It also usually shows up many times in a book. I went through the same process as above, emphasizing the word *the* and saying it with varying tones, silly antics, and funny faces. It wasn't long before they could "help" me read a book by reading all *the's*.

In the same manner, it is easy to find a frequently used word in a book and point out that word so they can begin to recognize it and "help" you read the book. We had a book about a girl who was learning to use the potty. She had to learn to sit for a long time for poo-poo to come out. One of the pages was completely filled with several lines of "...and sat and sat and sat and sat and sat and sat and sat..." Even before a kid recognizes words, they could "help" read *that* page! Engage them to interact with the book. This generates interest into books in general and sets your child up to desire to read by himself.

BEGINNING TO READ

It becomes only a matter of time before these consistent interactions with books, activities, and reinforcements translate into letter and word recognition. The question becomes: When do you take the next step into "formally" teaching them how to read? And then how do you put all the letters together to form words and teach them to spell?

Take your cue from your child. My oldest son was recognizing words at age two, "helping" me read by age three, reading with help at age four, and reading on his own in kindergarten. My youngest daughter was chomping at the bit by age four, but because of the short age gap and sensitivity of my middle child, I waited for my middle son to be ready before formally teaching my youngest to read. Instead, I challenged her with sight words from the Bible each Sunday, and she'd spend that week poring over a Bible and coming to show me what she'd found.

Though my middle son did not demonstrate a willingness to learn to read until he was nearly seven, when he finally approached me and wanted to read, he caught on quickly and learned to read in under two weeks. Who wouldn't want that?!? No tears or frustration, just an eagerness to learn because it's what he wanted to do. I didn't know it was even possible to learn that fast.

• • • • • • • • • • •

I never allowed reading to be a source of contention...only a source of pleasure.

• • • • • • • • • • •

I never allowed reading to be a source of contention, so it became only a source of pleasure. Both children devoured books at an unbelievable rate. When we moved back to the States, my daughter would check out fifty books a week from the library, so glad was she to have a variety of reading material.

BACK TO THE WHITEBOARD

I still marvel at how quickly and effortlessly my youngest two learned to read. What I'd dreaded with my middle son was a non-issue since I'd waited until he was ready and asking to learn. Using the whiteboard really helped in assisting his brain by using larger letters at first. From there, he transitioned painlessly into reading print. This is how I wish I'd learned to read!

Like all the other subjects, whatever reading program you decide upon is not nearly so important as when and how you implement it. The best program in the world can fail to bring about the desired or promised results if you push too quickly or too hard.

From my experience, I believe that the whiteboard can be a powerful tool in assisting the learning-to-read process. If I'd known about the whiteboard before South Korea, I would have used it in many ways before the children learned to read. I've included several of these ideas in the "Practical Tips & Ideas" section located at the back of this book.

WRITING AT THE WHITEBOARD

I also used the whiteboard to begin the writing process. It is a great starter tool. The larger markers make it easier to grip, and kids like the colors of dry erase markers. You can do it together at a larger board or use smaller personal boards.

It is important to teach the details of a letter the first time you walk them through it. Similar to my experience in teaching music, I found that it is a lot easier and less hassle to learn something right the first time than to struggle to relearn something after it has been practiced incorrectly. This one tip will save a lot of headache and stress while teaching your child how to form their letters for handwriting.

As you show them how to draw a letter, add a funny remark that you can refer to later as you continue practicing. "Here's how we make an *A*… We draw a line down this way, and a line down this way, and then we draw another line between the two. We always want to make sure these two lines at the top *touch and kiss. Mmmwah!*"

Think ahead to common mistakes, or areas that need special attention for correct formation. A common error is for an *A* to appear more like an *H* when the vertical lines are not connected. By adding a catchphrase, it brings humor and fun into the instruction as you help them draw the letter: "*Dowwwwn* this way, good. Now where do we start the next line? *Mmmmwah!* Yes, *A* likes to *kiss*. So, our lines have to be *touching*. Now *dowwwwn* the other way and connect the two in the middle. Great job!"

Provide the narrative as you write the letter together. First, use hand-over-hand. Next, demonstrate while they follow your lead. Then narrate while they try it themselves. Hearing it as they do it connects the catchphrase to the letter. After a while, swap to the student role and soft-test. "So, tell me how to make an *A*. What do I do first?" If they do not add the catchphrase and instruct you to touch the second line to the first line, make it more like an *H*. They will notice and immediately correct you. This is fun *and* instructive to their own learning and retention.

This same technique can be employed later for teaching cursive. The important thing is to practice without error from the beginning. Be there to offer step-by-step narration and immediate correction to the marker position before they even begin making a mistake. Practicing incorrectly results in the need for retraining muscle memory, which requires more patience than learning it right the first time.

DAILY MANAGEMENT

I have found all sorts of ways to use the whiteboard around the home. Depending on where it's located, you can use it for a variety of things.

In the kitchen or pertaining to the kitchen, you can use it for grocery lists. This can be hung on the door of a pantry, the side of the fridge, or a wall in the kitchen where the kids can add an item to the list when something runs out. It helps to teach them responsibility when emptying an item by learning about lists, and it gives them practice with handwriting and spelling.

In a common area of a room, I have one of my larger whiteboards where I include a weekly schedule, daily schedule, to-do list, personal section for each child, and a note section to myself. I like to divide and label these areas using wet erase markers which only erase with a wet cloth. This keeps them "permanent" so I can write and erase in the spaces freely with dry-erase markers.

I also incorporate colors. I buy the packs with the extra colors so I can assign everyone in the house a specific color, and also color-code events on the weekly schedule. At a glance without reading the details, I can get an idea about what is on the board. The same board, or a separate one, can be used specifically for school and chores.

The kids find the color coding helpful and pay attention to "their" color. They also pay attention to other significant colors, like red, reserved for "pay attention!" By using color, it allows the younger children who are not yet reading to be included in "reading" the board. Symbols can be used to teach color and shapes: a yellow star for church-related events, a green dot (circle) for school-related activities, a blue triangle for family-related outings, etc.

● ● ● ● ● ● ● ● ● ●

Using the board in the early years teaches the children to pay attention and take responsibility for themselves.

● ● ● ● ● ● ● ● ● ●

A picture of a dog followed by a dot in the child's color may be all you need to indicate to a non-reading child that they need to feed the dog. When they've completed the task, they get to put a checkmark beside it. Then, you can respond with a big smiley face. They love this.

Side bonus: When something is written down, it's harder to argue with. Having things written down in a visible place helps silence disagreements that arise from, "I thought you said," "I forgot you said," and "I didn't hear you say that," categories. In a sense, it backs up the authority of your word. It settles the issue.

This written way of communicating becomes invaluable as children get older. They will already be trained to pay attention to the board. This makes it really nice when you remember things after they've gone to bed. You can write it on the board knowing they'll read it when they wake up. And as they hit the mobile teen years, it's a great way to stay in communication with them.

Currently, I have four whiteboards hung in my house. One is in the office area with my to-do reminders and lists, one is in the main room with each child's name for communication, one is in the kitchen for grocery and to-buy lists, and one hangs on our upright freezer that lists daily and weekly chores, consequences, and privileges. I have two more that aren't hung up but get pulled out as needed for projects.

Whether it's for school, privileges, chores, or activity times, I love having the boards to go back to, refer to, and write quick reminders on. As my children get older, it's especially nice for communication when we don't see each other all day because of our separate schedules. And it's fun to write little notes to give encouragement and a smiley face.

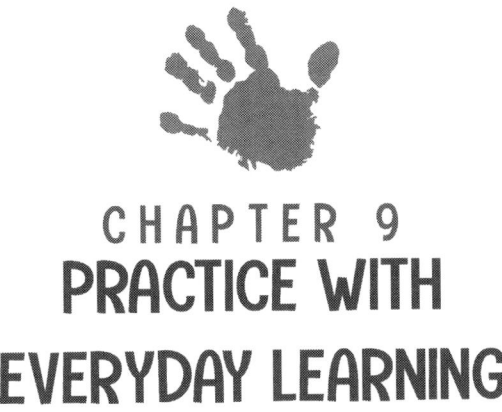

CHAPTER 9
PRACTICE WITH EVERYDAY LEARNING

I learned two principles that became basic for me and influenced my approach to schooling. They were from my early reading experience and later in my piano teaching days. First, to teach when the child is ready, not pushing ahead beforehand. Second, to teach them in life and practice first, then transition to paper. The power of learning by connecting a new concept to information they already hold is incredible.

PRACTICE BEFORE PAPER

I used to teach piano when I was in my teens. The method I taught advocated approaching music in a nontraditional manner. Rather than requiring the student to understand their staff and music notes before beginning to play, this approach concentrated on the student first playing the piano by sight and memorization.

After the first thirty-minute lesson, they would go home being able to play two songs, on both the black and white keys. Very quickly, they were playing all over the keyboard. They were always amazed at themselves and how easy it was to play the piano, and their parents were impressed!

I waited until the students had been playing awhile and were having fun before introducing them to the musical staff, traditional notes, and understanding the theory of what they were playing. They would at first be in shock and awe at seeing on paper what they had been effortlessly playing.

We still didn't play from any traditional music for several months, or even up to a year. When we finally made the change, it was not big or scary to them like it would have been in the beginning. They already knew how to play the piano, and they were comfortable with the keyboard. At that point, they were only learning on paper what they already knew how to do. From there, the door to all traditionally written music was open to them.

PRACTICE IN REAL LIFE

My kids were little helpers with baking before they could climb onto a chair. They helped prepare ingredients, dumped measurements into the bowls, cracked some eggs (in a separate small bowl at first), helped with the mixing, turned on the oven, set the timer, watched for the baking to be done, and were the first taste testers.

All of these things they first watched me do. I would invite them up on a chair to watch, then ask if they wanted to help. As they helped, I used big words, adult words, as I showed them what I was doing. I would define some of the big words for them. I would explain and describe what I was doing and why, but I didn't talk down to them. They felt quite grown up helping. And they loved to use the grown-up words they learned, too.

There came a point when they were no longer satisfied with my filling the measuring cups and their dumping it. They wanted to fill them, too. I would show them on the recipe the measurement needed. They were already familiar with the names of the measurements as I had called them by name each time I used them. Now I showed them on each measurement what to look for.

When they got a little older and knew all the measuring cups by name, I would do a little "water show" with them. I started with ½ cup, pouring the water into the 1 cup, since they were already familiar with the concept of "half." Then, I'd have them fill the ¼ cup into the ½ cup, and the ¼ cup into the ¾ cup, explaining the math as they did so. As they picked up the quarter cup fractions, I'd show them the ⅓ cup measurements. They understood they could fill the ⅓ cup twice or use the ⅔ cup.

After they became more independent and comfortable with the recipes we made often, I'd purposely request a double batch. When a recipe called for ⅔ cup, I'd show them how 4/3 cup was 1 cup with ⅓ left over, so it became 1⅓ cup.

As they became proficient in doubling recipes, I'd write out a doubled recipe ahead of time and tell them I only needed a half-batch. Again, I'd show them with the measurement cups how to cut the fractions in half. Sometimes we went back to the water demonstration to prove or disprove our answers.

While in grade school, all of my children were proficient with measurements, knives, cooking, and baking. They could hold their own in a kitchen. They worked alongside me or my husband with competence, and we had fun whipping up meals together.

I prefer to bake and follow a recipe. My husband likes to cook and be creative. The kids learned both. By their early teen years, I got kicked out of the kitchen quite often as they created all sorts of meals on their own. With the influence of living in Asia while they were young, they use a lot of fresh veggies and do a lot of chopping.

My kids have long surpassed and now challenge me in the cooking department. My second son especially can turn out an amazingly tasty five-star dish, complete with garnish, color, and balance of taste. He can even make Brussels sprouts taste good! He rarely uses a recipe, and when he does, he always tweaks it. My daughter makes her own delicious alfredo sauce, making other restaurants' pasta pale in comparison. The last time my oldest son was home from college, he and I created a recipe together based on his idea for a stuffed grilled burger. It impressed even my second son, which said a lot.

• • • • • • • • • • • •

You don't have to know how to do something very well in order to give your child a taste and let them develop their own interests.

• • • • • • • • • • • •

Just include them in doing things, offer them opportunities, and give them a chance to practice their growing skills. They will make messes, but that's to be expected. Simply teach them how to clean up their mess. They'll either be more careful, or they won't mind cleaning up after themselves.

TRANSITIONING TO PAPER

When the time came to learn basic fractions in math, all I needed to do was refer to baking. They already understood the concepts. Fractions were a breeze. Long before the math books introduced adding and subtracting fractions, they were doubling and halving recipes. At first, the scene at the table usually looked something like this:

The kids looked at the new material and start to come unglued. "Oh, this looks *hard!*" they'd moan, looking up in desperation.

"Nonsense!" I immediately replied. "This is easy! You already know your fractions. Remember when we bake and you use the ½ cup, ⅔ cup, and the ¾ teaspoon? Remember how we double a recipe? All the book is doing now is showing you how it looks on paper. You already know how to do this, so you'll catch on lickity-split. It'll be super easy and you'll wonder why you ever thought it was hard."

After this pep talk, I'd get the measurements out and connect what they already knew to what the paper was showing them. "Ohhhhhh, *that's* all this is?" they'd ask. "This is easy! I thought it would be hard. This won't take long at all to get done."

As time went on and more new material and concepts came up in the math book, the initial responses began to change. "This looks hard, but I bet it turns out to be easy like the other times. It's probably something we already know, right, Mom?"

"That's right. You'll catch on in no time. No problem!"

Even if I hadn't quite gotten to a concept before it came up in the book, I would always find a way to connect it to something they were already familiar with. Then, even if I introduced the topic right then, it still didn't seem hard because they associated it with something they already knew.

Decimals were one such item. They understood about money, knew how to write out dollar amounts, but had not yet realized that the "dot" was a decimal point. When the word and concept for decimal was introduced, I got out some money and showed them the correlation. Adding and subtracting decimals was the same. Out came the bills and coins. And as always … it was "easy."

MOUNTAIN OR MOLEHILL

Attitude trumps everything. If your own attitude is right, you have a good chance of changing their opinion about something being hard. But if you already believe something will be difficult, it will be like climbing up Mount Everest. Even if they have the ability, if they do not hold the belief and confidence that they can learn it and it can be easy, it's a steep climb to the top.

● ● ● ● ● ● ● ● ● ● ●

> **Your attitude is like a ski lift. It makes the ride to the top quicker, more enjoyable, and a lot less energy-consuming.**

● ● ● ● ● ● ● ● ● ● ●

Once they reach the summit of learning new material, they can have fun breezing through the problems in the book, feeling the triumph of achievement and victory as they reach the bottom of the page and are done for the day.

I had a variety of go-to statements that essentially pointed to the same idea and repeated a central theme: school is easy, learning is fun. "This is really easy. You're going to get it right away." "Let me show you on paper what you already know!" "This will be fun. It's super easy." "I love ___. It's really fun!"

I always spoke confidence toward their ability to learn and catch on quickly. And when it was something I also really enjoyed, I shared that, too. Be intentional about being contagious in a good way.

Something that will quickly make a mountain out of a molehill is to push a lot of paperwork. Paperwork for paperwork's sake should not be required, especially before they really understand the concept. A lack of relevance results in a lack of interest, with disastrous results of being overwhelmed and having a bad attitude towards the subject.

REMEMBER THE POINT

There are times you may need to ask yourself, "What is the point?" Good question. What *is* the point? Whatever you are doing, whether it is home or school related, it is always worth knowing its relevance.

Don't be a bully.

If you're only doing something just to satisfy a curriculum or because it's what someone else does, think again and reconsider. If you know there *is* a point, but you don't know what it is, then learn it so you can show your child why. Google it. If you still cannot explain it, then find someone who can.

If you realize that you've been doing something for the wrong reasons, the answer is easy. Acknowledge it to your child, apologize, and stop. There's no point in pressuring or pushing something, especially when it brings strife into the home.

If it's something you would really like to keep doing, but want to continue doing it for the right reasons, make sure those reasons are understood and clear. Give your child permission to respectfully call you out if you slip into old habits. Allow them to give you feedback and watch their willingness to work with you grow. Children provide very good accountability when you allow it.

It is important to the relationship between you and your child that you operate in your position of teacher with honor and virtue. Lead by example with integrity. Be a woman of grace, modeling the values you want to grow in them. Your children need this from you for more than their academic health.

CHAPTER 10
PERSONALIZED CURRICULUM, GRADING, & TESTING

Education is not a god. It is a tool. It is a very good tool and complements life when wielded in the right way. However, it can be ineffective and cause immense pain otherwise. Education and learning are designed to continue lifelong, not end at graduation. The goal is not only to prepare for graduation, but to prepare for being a learner for the rest of our lives.

HOMESCHOOL FREEDOM

Learning is not restricted to what we find in books and curriculum. The most important learning is about life, what it's about, our place in life, and our calling in it. This includes attitudes, beliefs, relationships, and ambition. Curriculum is built on these elements. When they are missing, curriculum alone cannot adequately prepare one for life. It cannot be isolated and taught separately.

Take hold of the freedom you have to school your children at home by giving them the personalizing they need to flourish and succeed. Too many homeschoolers follow the mainstream mindset of public and private schools with schedules, teaching format, and daily work and testing requirements.

You have the space and capacity as a homeschool mom to take advantage of opportunities and privileges available to individualize your child's school experience. You have the benefit of creativity, originality, and flexibility like none other. Leverage everything possible in helping your child excel in academics.

LEARNING IS THE GOAL

• • • • • • • • • •

There is no perfect system or curriculum except the one that is right and works for you and your child.

• • • • • • • • • •

Don't become a prisoner or slave to someone else's ideas or ideals. View any book requirement as a suggestion or an invitation to the author's opinion, and tailor your own requirements according to your child's needs and strengths. Remember, you are the teacher and the book is a tool.

PERSONALIZED CURRICULUM, GRADING, & TESTING

I would look through the books I chose and decide what parts of the text I would require, according to three standards: what was best for my child, what would keep them motivated, and what were their learning and testing styles. It differed sometimes from subject to subject. In some subjects I planned to finish the book, while in other subjects I chose the chapters or portions of a chapter I wanted to cover. In some subjects and days' lessons, I required every problem; others I didn't.

In one particular subject, spelling, I went above and beyond the book's requirements. I did so to ensure that my children truly learned the content and didn't just memorize it in order to pass. I chose to test them, both orally and in written form, to make sure they really understood.

Each week's lesson introduced new vocabulary words. I followed the book's recommended steps on how to learn new words. For the testing at the end of the week, however, I required a verbal test of the new words in addition to the written test provided. They usually scored higher in one or the other. I challenged all my children this way. We are generally better at one than the other, and I wanted to stimulate both areas of the brain regarding words.

In addition, I required the children to create a sentence using each new word they had learned. While they were younger, I required it in written form for handwriting practice. As they got older, they gave it orally. I detected their level of understanding for the new word by how they used it in the sentence. If they could memorize the spelling of new words, but they didn't know how to use them accurately, it did them little good. If that was the case, then what was the point of pushing the learning of new words?

An enhanced vocabulary is the bedrock to well-developed speaking and comprehension. It has enabled my children to be articulate and effective in their communication and has supported their success in following their desires.

However, during that season my children often complained about my super-strict (and in their minds, unnecessary) spelling requirements. But now they thank me for it. We laughed when my middle son returned to public school and his teacher also required both a written and oral test. He was sure only his mother was so unreasonable.

Just as a child does not comprehend the value of saving money when it is hindering him from the immediate gratification of spending it, so also a child will have difficulty appreciating additional curriculum requirements, especially when it keeps him from running outdoors to play.

In personalizing the curriculum, my goal was for results in competence, excellence, and confidence. When I required more than the curriculum book itself did, it was for a worthwhile and valid reason. You must keep in mind what is important to you for your child to learn. You must have a firm belief about what you are requiring and why. If you're not sure, search it out and be prayerful about it.

PAPER IN MODERATION

On the flip side, there were subjects I required far less than the book recommended or provided for. Don't make finishing every problem the goal just for the sake of it. Once they've learned a

PERSONALIZED CURRICULUM, GRADING, & TESTING

concept, there is no need to hammer them with busy work, unless they enjoy it.

• • • • • • • • •

Remember, the target is to learn, not to finish a book or a page.

• • • • • • • • •

The less time they have to sit trapped behind a table or desk, the better. And the more quickly they can complete their necessary paperwork, the happier they'll be.

In my earlier years, using the curriculum my parents chose, I was required to finish every problem in every book. By my high school years, I was allowed to complete every other problem in math and still meet the curriculum's requirements. One thing I noted from this experience is how much better I actually did when not forced to complete every problem. It was motivating and not nearly so overwhelming.

I also found improved performance and a better attitude in my own children with fewer requirements on paper. Of course, there is a reasonable and necessary amount of paperwork required for what needs to be learned. But a lot of books include plenty of extra problems for practice and review. This is a great resource, but it is not necessary to make your child complete repetitive work in order to measure their skills.

When we learned a new concept, I had them complete every other problem. If they demonstrated good understanding, that satisfied me and they did not have to finish the rest of the problems. For the remainder of the lesson, they had to complete one review problem for each of the previous lessons and concepts.

If they did not get a review problem right, then another similar problem was assigned. Sometimes they got a review problem wrong because we needed to brush up on a concept. But often, it was because they were rushing too quickly and needed to learn to be more careful and diligent in their homework. By receiving an extra problem for sloppy or careless work, they learned that responsibility and integrity also applied to their schoolwork.

"SOFT" TESTING WITHOUT ANXIETY

After introducing concepts in daily life, I would often "soft" test my children before transitioning to learning and testing on paper. I would measure their understanding by casually asking questions while doing a project together. In this way, I was able to get a feel for where they were at, which is the point of a test, without their being hampered by any testing anxiety.

Let me give a couple examples. While baking cookies together, the recipe may call for $\frac{2}{3}$ cup of sugar. When they pull out the $\frac{2}{3}$ cup measure, I would ask, "If that cup was dirty already, which other one could you use to measure out the sugar?" They look in the drawer, find the $\frac{1}{3}$ cup and reply, "This one."

"How?" I ask, digging for details.

"Well, I'd just put in two of them."

"That's right. Good job!" I respond. I've just laid the groundwork for when they encounter adding fractions on paper. And it gives me something to refer back to, letting them know that they already know these things, now they're going to learn them on paper.

We could be doubling a recipe together and when we get to 2 tablespoons, I can ask how else we can measure 4 tablespoons. Yes, a ¼ cup! Conversions are never hard when they are first learned in doing, not on paper. Paper gives the child no frame of reference.

In the same scenario, I can ask the child what would happen if we forgot to double the eggs, or didn't put the baking powder in. Though they will not immediately use this knowledge on paper, it will play a role in the future with science and chemistry. The more they know and can absorb through daily life, the more you will have to refer to, making school on paper less intimidating and more applicable.

When we corresponded with a friend from Japan and they told us that their temperature was 21 degrees Celsius, I would ask the children if they remembered what that is now in Fahrenheit. It's about 70 degrees. They didn't need to know the conversion equation yet. I let them know that there was a way to switch temperatures and that we'd learn it later. For now, they just knew some of the basic temperatures to get an idea of hot, cold, and comfortable. Later, as we learned it in the books, they understood the application for the equation process. I didn't hear the words, "Why do we have to learn this, Mom?" They already knew why.

While measuring wood or material for a project, I'd include all sorts of teaching and soft testing. Measuring to hang a picture or move furniture also works well. A yard stick and measuring tape are good tools. I'd do the same with a ruler when cutting 8.5 x 11 paper down to squares for origami. I'd also show them the odometer in the van, and we'd have a game guessing about how far it was between places. Sometimes just in the parking lot. How many tenths of a mile? This helps them understand distance and will prepare them for learning decimals in the future. It will make the learning relevant, pertinent, and useful.

Developing and remaining in the habit of questioning your child's knowledge in a relaxed, laid-back way is super helpful on so many levels. It allows you to more effectively guide them in their learning. You can successfully spark their interest, yet not overwhelm or bore them. You can help them see the connections between life and their schoolbooks. This makes learning more fun and meaningful.

It also helps them overcome their fear of answering questions. When making questions a normal pattern of everyday life, they learn to stop, think, and answer without fear of repercussions. They beam at your praise, and their creativity and personality show up in their answers. They also will become more comfortable with questions directed at them by other adults.

This is a huge plus, as it enables them to communicate and be assertive with other adults in a positive, respectful manner. Eventually, it will also prepare them for future interactions in interviews, with supervisors, and while working on the job.

As you introduce learning on paper and crack open the curriculum, it is important that your attitude precedes their learning. As I've mentioned before, be intentional about how you speak, how you approach the topic, and how you lead with your own attitude. If you are not in a good frame of mind, it's better to wait. You set the tone and atmosphere for learning. Remember, where there is strife is every evil thing. Peace is more effective.

PERSONALIZED "HARD" TESTING

I liked to incorporate different ways to test my children. Sometimes this was for the benefit of learning, like with spelling. Other times, it was to correspond with my child's learning styles. Knowing how your child operates best and understanding their learning styles will help you choose testing styles that are more comfortable for them and more effective in giving you a true picture of the knowledge they hold and are able to apply.

Your tests can be any form of oral, written, demonstrative, or a combination. You can tweak them however you need to best suit your purposes and what you want to glean. Depending on your child's preferences and strengths, add or mix testing styles. Sometimes, like with math, I would include all styles in order to test their strengths in varying ways.

Say they were learning simple addition. I'd get out pennies and do practical testing. Pushing two sets of coins forward, I'd ask, "What is 1 plus 3? 2 plus 4? 5 plus 2? 4 plus 5?" I'd start slow, giving them time, then slowly increase my speed in switching out the pennies to be added together. As they'd advance, I'd use nickels, dimes, and quarters to help with mental math. I'd also switch it up by calling out a number and having them form two piles of pennies which added up to the number.

Then I would give a flash card test. We'd keep track of their quickest daily score and their weekly progress. At first, I'd allow up to three misses to score, then slowly decrease to 100% accuracy. I would also do two short written tests, one untimed and one timed. Usually they were problems I had handwritten on blank paper, sprinkling in easy-peasy problems along with newer ones that challenged them.

● ● ● ● ● ● ● ● ● ●

You can learn a lot about your child when you utilize a variety of tests.

● ● ● ● ● ● ● ● ● ●

When you choose to use tests they do well in, it helps boost their confidence and morale. They can see their own growth and what they do well in. By using testing methods that challenge them, it shows you both places for improvement and gives them a chance to practice and develop weaker areas.

All of the test variants may be accomplished in a short amount of time. Rather than being overwhelming or something to dread, the assessments are a place of excited accomplishment and success. But this environment was not automatic. I was intentional about the atmosphere of testing I created.

First, I would give a compliment, followed by what I noticed they did right. Only then would I point out what they needed to work on, followed up with a statement of confidence in their abilities to make the needed improvements. "You've got this!" or "I know you can do this" goes a long way. Even if they really blew it, there was usually something they'd done right.

This is true for your child, too. Search for what they do right, and mention that first. Always celebrate the success and point out where they are improving, especially when they feel disappointed about their own performance.

My middle son would often feel discouraged if he didn't beat his previous score. I would point out that even though he took a few seconds longer, he got only two wrong instead of three this time. Or even though he took longer, he got the new, more difficult math problems correct, so that was progress. If he just really bombed it, I'd offer a re-do, which he generally chose.

Your response to their work affects their future work and attitude. Always be their cheerleader, advocate, and encouragement. Keep the testing quick, fun, and positive. The more "short-quiz" type testing you do, the less they will dread tests in general. Be intentional about building a healthy context around testing. Acknowledge what they need to work on but give more attention to what they do well.

BENEATH THE SURFACE

If your child has just flat out done a poor job and has a negative attitude, stop. I promise you, it's not about the homework or test. It's not about their ability to understand or learn. Something else is going on that is affecting them. You need to get to the bottom of what is really bothering them before you move on. Forget the test or daily work for a moment and give them your full attention. Whatever is blocking their performance needs to be addressed. I would immediately turn to them and ask, "What's going on?" I'd pursue until I learned what was afflicting them that was affecting their schoolwork.

It often had little to do with school or the actual content. There was something that needed to be resolved before they were able to fully concentrate. It was something to do with our daily life or their lack of confidence in their ability.

● ● ● ● ● ● ● ● ●

The brain thinks and operates best when it is at peace, both with itself and others around them.

● ● ● ● ● ● ● ● ●

Sometimes my daughter was lambasting herself mentally. She needed truth spoken to her. She needed to hear my reassurance and to get a hug. Sometimes my son was upset with me about something that happened that morning or the night before. We would talk it out and deal with it so that peace was restored.

One way that helped me recognize if the problem was non-school related was to compare their current work against their usual work. It would tip me off if they missed several review answers when they normally only missed a couple. If their handwriting was sloppy when it was normally neat, I knew something else was going on. Handwriting was an accurate barometer for my children's emotions. So was the number of "easy mistakes." Their concentration was obviously elsewhere, or they were down in the dumps about something.

One thing was certain, they were not fully concentrating or at peace within themselves. This was proven so many times it became uncontestable in our household. When I noticed an increase in mistakes or decrease in legible handwriting, I called a halt and we stopped to talk about what was going on. This beat bickering over school content and developing discord between us.

In order to resume and bring peace, we found that sometimes a simply put, yet heartfelt, affirmation or apology was all it took to turn things around quickly. Afterwards, when your child proceeds with their studies, you'll be amazed at how much better they do. Don't miss the relational aspect and get stuck focusing on their performance.

LETTER GRADES VS. TRUE UNDERSTANDING

You have a choice as to how you grade through daily work and tests. You have a choice in what you focus on. My mom used letter grades, per the requirements from the curriculum she was using. Because those letter grades meant the world to her, they were also what I focused on. I knew the expectation was the A-B range, so that is what I aimed for.

The achievement of a higher letter grade was not always attained with peace or a sense of accomplishment, however. It was often performance driven, and I didn't always retain what I'd memorized for the test. In fact, I struggled with wanting to cheat when I wasn't understanding the content.

● ● ● ● ● ● ● ● ● ●

I wanted three things more than letter grades for my children: quality, responsibility, and understanding.

● ● ● ● ● ● ● ● ● ●

I wanted them to give their best and to be responsible for understanding what they were learning. I didn't want them defining and comparing themselves by their grades and performance, especially since I had two who were so night and day different.

When I graded, I would give credit for how many they got right. As I handed them a test, I'd say something like, "Let's see how many you get right on the first try." If there were ten math problems, and they missed two, I would write +8/10 at the top. Their goal was 10/10, but it was from a positive place rather than a negative one.

Then, the grading didn't stop there. I always required a 10/10 for completion. Whatever they missed, they had to correct. If their score was +4/10, I'd tell them "good job" on the four done well, and then advise them to slow down and concentrate as they corrected the remaining six. When they turned the paper back in and had a +9/10, I'd congratulate them and say, "Great job! You only have one more to correct and then you'll be finished."

This approach provided the motivation to do a good job the first time around. They knew if they rushed through their work, they'd just have to do it again. It was an incentive to avoid repeat grading. It also reduced the amount of frustration for both them and me. Rather than being disheartened because they "weren't getting it," we celebrated as they "got it right."

This approach also helped me detect if an attitude was affecting them. If they repeatedly made a lot of mistakes or did a poor job, they knew we'd be pausing to have a little talk. If they were just being stubborn, it helped me to keep a positive attitude and not respond to them in kind.

POSITIVE GRADING

In addition to grading with a focus on how many items were correct, I learned a few more ways to make grading more positive. No one likes to see big red X's or corrective marks on their paper. One of the things I changed was to use different colored markers for grading, not red. Red makes a statement, and usually not an encouraging one.

Second, instead of marking an incorrect problem with an X, I began marking each correct problem with a checkmark. The goal was a full page of checkmarks. Rather than scanning the paper for what they did wrong, the children first got to see all the checkmarks for what they did right. It also helped me know where I had graded if I got interrupted mid-page.

Once all re-dos were finished and everything was checkmarked, I added something that we picked up in Japan. I would draw a big circle around the page, swirling smaller and smaller a couple of times as I circled inward, creating a spiral. It indicated that the paper was completed to satisfaction. Done. The kids loved this.

The point to positive grading is to keep their identity grounded on who they really are and not based on their abilities…to be rooted in true understanding and a working knowledge, not on performance. Be careful that a focus on performance is not what forms your child's identity about who they are.

> **You can definitely expect a good job, but separate out who they are from how they perform.**

Don't wrap up who they are into how they perform with school. I had one firm rule of thumb: "attitude above all." Attitude comes from a choice of mindset that shapes our integrity, character, and honor.

AM I ON TRACK?

I know what you may be asking. If you don't give traditional letter grades, how can you know where your child is academically? I promise, you will have a very good feel for how your child is doing by how they complete their work and demonstrate their understanding, as I described above. This is how I graded until they hit high school, when I gave letter grades with a modified approach.

I was given letter grades and standardized testing every year. I graduated a year early and did well on my ACT for college. My children were never given traditional letter grades until high school. They did no standardized testing while homeschooling. My oldest son graduated a year and a half early. My daughter graduated two years early. My middle son happily finished on time. They all did well on their ACT/SAT college entrance testing.

PERSONALIZED CURRICULUM, GRADING, & TESTING

My point? It doesn't matter. If you want to test your child for your own peace of mind, go ahead. But if you don't, you will not cause their academic shipwreck. As confirmed by Finland, standardized testing is not necessary for excellence.

Here's a secret: every curriculum varies in its approach. They also vary in the timing recommended for teaching their material. Each curriculum will ultimately reach the same goals. The middle ground is a place of incongruency that will eventually sort itself out. Therefore, don't compare what your child knows with what another child knows. Even if you're using the same curriculum, you should each be going according to your child's ability and readiness.

CHAPTER 11
MEETING YOUR GOALS

The days may seem long right now as you struggle to balance life and school. But the day is coming when your little tykes will be taller than you, they won't feel they need you, and they will consider themselves all grown up as they go off to college. Believe me, that day will come more quickly than you'll ever be ready for.

• • • • • • • • •

How you relate with your young-adult children will be based on how you relate with them right now.

• • • • • • • • •

It is important to keep long-range goals in sight as well as the shorter-range ones. Long-range goals help us to adjust our mindsets and priorities. They give us the strength for the day-to-day grind and the courage to make necessary changes. They reset our navigation when we can't see the forest for the trees, and they remind us that we need to pace ourselves because we are running a marathon, not a sprint, with our children. When the unexpected or undesired happens, we can be flexible and modify our approach while readjusting back toward our long-term goals.

LOOKING AHEAD IN LIFE AND SCHOOL

As a young mother, I watched other families interact with their children and I came to some conclusions and long-range goals for the relationships I wanted with my own children. First, I never bought into the "terrible twos" idea. I saw the potential in two-year-olds, and at this stage, as they started interacting, things got interesting and fun. I called them the "terrific twos," and my first long-range goal was to enjoy the terrific twos with my child, using it to lay a foundation for future relationships with my child.

The second thing that bothered me was the many fractured relationships I saw between teens and parents. I had the unique experience of hosting a foreign exchange student during her senior year while my own children were six and three. She spoke highly of her parents, and treated my husband and I with respect, even through conversations involving conflict. I was highly impressed and glad to see that relationship during the teen years was possible. That became my next long-term goal.

Having those two goals required maintaining a positive mindset. Many times I had to have an attitude adjustment in order to move forward toward my goals. Life challenged me. The children challenged me. My emotions challenged me. Each time, I made the decision to either hold fast to my goal or to believe my current circumstances and give up.

I'm so glad I persevered. I have relationships with my young-adult children that I am grateful for, beyond what I thought possible at their ages. They have been through a lot and overcome many things in life, and I am proud of them. They have each exceeded my expectations and I am excited to see what is ahead for them in the future.

Academically, my mom's biggest goal for her children was for us to graduate with better grades than she did. We all did that. She wanted to help us successfully pursue our dreams and goals. She did that. I wanted to personalize and individualize my children's education experience. I did that. I wanted them to demonstrate integrity, godly morals, and a hard work ethic above academics. They do this.

For both my mom and I, we held long-term goals and dreams that we began pursuing with our children while they were young. This provided patterns that continued as they got older and grew into adulthood. The ways in which you choose to relate with your children while they are still young impacts them greatly.

FOR A LIFETIME

The most memorable point I hope I've made in this book is that learning is first and foremost a way of life, and that it should continue throughout our lives.

● ● ● ● ● ● ● ● ●

> **Learning is a way of life that should continue throughout our lives.**

● ● ● ● ● ● ● ● ●

Therefore, your job as mother and teacher is never "done." You will always be teaching your children. Your choice will be about how intentional you are with what you teach, but they will certainly pick up on what they watch in your interactions and relationships with them and with others.

My youngest two are now entering adulthood. My oldest is no longer a teen. He comes home to visit over the summer and holidays. I've found that several things I've shared with you in this book are still applicable to a young-adult household and continue to work well. As your children become young adults, they will still have different needs and approach life in different ways. Put forth the effort now to respect their individual ways of learning, support their personal goals, and honor them as their own individual. When you do this, they will come back to you for advice and input. The way they receive information remains similar, and they still have different needs that you will need to respect.

PRIORITIES

Your beliefs and attitudes matter more than you know. Be intentional about the patterns you generate. Have clear goals for what you want and be honest with yourself. Your goals will affect your expectations and heart toward your children. Make sure the goals are also respectful and honoring to both you and your child.

I am convinced that whatever is important to you, whatever your personal goals with your children are, you can attain. Don't let others tell you what is possible for you and your family. Press forward with God and you will succeed.

TIPS & STRATEGIES
CREATIVE TEACHING IN DAILY LIFE

The following section is here to provide you with practical ideas and examples for introducing different subjects in fun, applicable, and effective ways. They are suggestions to help stimulate your creative juices and help you insert the "home" in homeschool.

I came to realize the value of the whiteboard out of necessity in South Korea. If I had recognized it earlier, I would have used it from the time my toddlers were youngsters. In the following sections, I've included ideas that I would have used if I had known about the whiteboard earlier on.

PHONICS & READING

TIPS

- ✎ Since reading requires interaction with books, start that interaction as soon as possible.
- ✎ Gain their interest in connecting with books by reading, singing, coloring, play-acting, book-on-CD, etc. Use topics they are interested in.
- ✎ Continue daily interaction with books through pre-school.
- ✎ Take your cues from your child…don't be afraid to wait until they want to read (this diminishes the struggle, since the desire to learn is present).
- ✎ Use the whiteboard to work with letters, letter sounds, and initial words.
- ✎ I give examples in learning to read in Chapter 8—Wonders of the Whiteboard.

I came to realize the value of the whiteboard out of necessity in South Korea. If I had recognized it earlier, I would have used it from the time my toddlers were youngsters. I found it to be very effective for teaching. In this section, I include ideas that I would have used if I'd known then what I know now.

BOOKS

- Babies
    - Sing nursery rhyme books.

- If you can talk, you can sing. Don't worry about being off-tune. When I didn't know a nursery rhyme tune, I made one up—not necessarily creatively, just sing-songy.
- Young Toddlers
  - Read all sorts of books—discover their initial areas of interest.
  - Read books on all early learning topics: alphabet, numbers, colors, shapes, and foods.
  - Read picture dictionaries to expand their vocabulary and knowledge.
  - Read about subjects from their little world, like potty training, getting a new sister, dressing themselves, going to church, etc.
- Older Toddlers
  - Continue reading books to broaden your child's areas of interest.
  - Expand reading library to include areas like critical thinking, personal hygiene, manners and etiquette, character qualities, emotions, personal safety, and sharing.
  - Include rhyming and poem books—this helps with cognitive development and experiencing the rhythm of language. They learn to anticipate the rhyming word which sets you up later to have them "help" you read the book.
  - Introduce magazines (another type of reading material) into their world.

- Preschool
    - Introduce new areas of widening interest.
    - Include books on various areas of safety: body boundaries, strangers, road safety, fire safety, electrical safety, safety in public, etc.
    - Read "how-to" books: how skyscrapers are built, how a caterpillar becomes a butterfly, how our bodies work, how to mix primary colors, etc.
    - Introduce preschool-level magazines with activities and experiments to do together.

EARLY PHONETICS AND SOUND CORRELATIONS

- Emphasize a sound and make a correlation with the sound.
    - "Mmmm, this is an apple. *A-a-apple.*"
    - "Emma, *E-E-Emma*. What else starts with *e*? *E-eggs, e-elephant, e-envelope.*"
    - "Let's run down to the mailbox, *r-r-run!—rrrright* now!"
- Do actions that match a sound. Say the sounds as you do the actions.
    - Jump! *J-j-jump!* Hop! *H-h-hop!* Skip! *Sk-sk-skip!*
    - Duck—*d-d-duck!* Crawl—*c-c-crawl.* Roll—*r-r-roll.*
    - *T-t-tiptoe. Wh-wh-whisper.*
- Silly Singing
    - Make up songs about what you're doing, beginning with easy tunes, to nursery songs. Emphasize sounds

as you go. Ad lib from there—go for it! The following are examples for practicing *e's* and *r's* separately, then together. Simply stress the letter sound in the sentence that you are silly-singing.

- "We're gon-na *eeeeeat, eeeeeat, eeeeeeat,* Cheer-i-os and pret-zels!" (from *I Like to Eat Apples and Bananas*)
- "This is the way we *brrrrrush* our teeth, *brrrrrush* our teeth, *brrrrrrush* our teeth." (from *Here We Go 'Round the Mulberry Bush*)
- "This *grrrrreen* bean, he's been cooked. He's been cooked for us to *eeeeeat*. So we'll *eeeeeeat* him down with a yum-my chomp-chomp...this *grrrrreen* bean is now all gone!" (from *This Old Man*)
- Making references back to nursery rhyme songbooks by singing ditties like these strengthens the ties and interest in the books.

LETTER ACTIVITIES

Fridge Magnets

- Free play with the letters.
- Arrange into ABC order and sing the alphabet.
- Pick-a-Letter: while in the kitchen, separate out a letter as you make a connection to what you're doing.
    - While cutting an apple for a snack: separate the *A*, point it out, and say, "*A* is for apple!" Or give it to them to hold

while you cut the apple. Afterwards, have them "put the *A*-for-apple back on the fridge while we go eat our apple."

- While washing dishes, separate the *D* and do the same. "We'll put the *D* for dishes right here until we get done." Then, "*D-d-done* with *d-d-dishes*! We can put the *d-d-D* back with his friends now."

- As they recognize letters, ask them to pick out the letter for you. "While I'm making the oatmeal, can you find the *O* for oatmeal? *Ooooatmeal*." And, "Let's find the *S* for sweep as we sweep the floor. *Ssssweep*."

Find-a-Letter

- Hide a letter somewhere on the fridge or other metal surface in the kitchen. "Where's the *Y*? Can you find the *Y*?"

- Play Find-a-Letter game: name a letter for them to find or to find together.

- Reverse Find-a-Letter game: have them name a letter for you to find. Sometimes pick the wrong one and ask, "Is this the *H*? Look at it together… "Nooooo!" Pick another. "Hmmm…is this the *H*?—yes!" They love it when you are occasionally "wrong" and you find the answer together or they are able to correct you.

Food Fun

- Create letters out of food items like pancakes, finger jello, animal cracker letters, pretzels, snack pieces, etc.

- Make letters by eating strategic portions of a piece of food. Eating an *L* or a *T* out of a half piece of toast or eating a whole piece of toast into a circle or *O*. An *S* can also be formed from toast, though it is a bit trickier. On the other hand, an *S* can be formed by eating two half slices of an orange (shaped like *c*'s) and putting the rind halves together in opposing directions.

- Arrange letters out of snacks like Cheerios, raisins, peanuts, etc.
- Noodle Doodle: Practice forming letters out of cooked noodles. They are flexible enough to make any shape, and fun to eat afterwards, especially with dipping sauces.
- Eating Games: Have fun eating letters and show them how some letters turn into other letters as you eat them.
    - "I'm eating the *P*. Oh-no, I ate his leg! Now he looks like a *D*!"
    - Make a pancake in the shape of an *8* and show them how to nibble on it to make an *S*.
    - Demonstrate how some lowercase letters swap to become a different letter. "I'm going to eat a *b*." (Flip it mirror image.) "No, I changed my mind, I'm going to eat a *d*. (Flip it upside down.) "Hmmm, actually, I'm going to eat a *p*."
    - Eating upper case: A→V, B→P, E→F, I→T, M→N, O→C, O→U, P→D, Q→O, R→K, S→C, W→V, X→Y, Z→V.
    - Eating lower case: d→a, e→c, j→i, m→n, o→c, o→u, s→c, u→r.
    - Flip/rotating letters: H↔I, N↔Z, b↔d, b↔q, d↔p, t↔x, u↔n.

Matching Games

- Use two decks of letter cards. Match upper case↔upper case, lower case↔lower case, and upper case↔lower case.
- Line the cards into a shape of interest as you match them up (a "snake"/"giant noodle" line, a "cage"/"house" square, a "spider"/"flower" circle).
- Play the "Memory" game with letter cards.
- Hide some letters and have them play hide-n-seek. Afterwards, sing the alphabet and arrange the letters in alphabetical order.
- Tape some letters on the wall (or play at the table). Have them slap the matching letter you hold up.

Whiteboard Activities

- Write the alphabet on the board.
  - Point to each letter as you sing the ABCs.
  - Have them help you point to each letter as you sing.
  - Have them point to each letter as you sing.
- Point out a letter they are learning while you write a note on the board. I often did this while writing out my grocery list, but a board makes the letters bigger to see and easier to recognize.
- Write a letter on the board. Have them guess it.
- Write a bunch of letters on the board and have them point to, circle, or erase each letter as you name it.
- Do upper case, then lower case, then mixed cases.

- Write two columns of letters—one upper case and one lower case. Have them draw lines matching the letters.
- Use two colors to strengthen color recognition and help differentiate between upper case and lower case letters.

Games-on-the-Go

- What-Starts-With game: (while driving)
    - Pick a letter and point out things you see that start with that letter.
    - Point out things you see and figure out what letter it starts with.
    - Going through the alphabet, find something that starts with each letter.
    - Going through the alphabet, take turns finding something that starts with the letter. (I see an airplane, my son sees a bird, my daughter sees a car, etc.)
    - Name a letter and then see who can be the first to spot something starting with that letter.
- Billboard & Sign game: (while driving)
    - From billboards and signs of all types, point out big alphabet letters they are learning.
    - Going through the alphabet, find the letters in order.
    - Race to see who finishes first in spotting the alphabet in order.
    - Best suited for driving through town or while traveling through large cities.

- License Plate Game: (while driving)
    - Similar to the Billboard & Sign game, except you are limited to license plates. This is a progression from the Billboard & Sign game because the letters are smaller and more difficult to recognize.
    - Best suited for country driving or interstate travel.
- More Letter Activities:
    - While grocery shopping, name each item and the letter it starts with as you put it in the cart.
    - While in a store, point out items and figure out what letter they start with.
    - During a church service, write down a letter and have your child find 5 of them in the Bible. Or, write down a group of letters and have them find one of each and check them off.
    - In a large enough area, scuffle your feet to "draw" a letter in the dirt, sand, or gravel.
    - Play follow the leader and "walk out" a letter. Or create a letter and walk on it: arrange sticks or leaves outside into a large *M*, or use paper pieces or sticky notes indoors to create "dotted" letters to walk over.

WORKING WITH WORDS

Your child doesn't have to be reading or spelling independently in order to do the following activities. Just getting them more comfortable in working with letters in the context of words is of great value and benefit.

PHONICS & READING

It helps to familiarize and prepare them for the process of linking letters and eventually forming words. It takes the "scary" out of words further down the road.

Working with words also increases their awareness that you are reading *words* when you read them a book. These words are what make a book interesting. It will simply be a measure of time before they are interested enough in these words that they will want to read them for themselves.

FRIDGE MAGNETS

- Create-a-Word: similar to Pick-a-Letter, form a word in connection with what you are doing in the kitchen, sounding out the letters as you form it.
    - Pick out, then arrange the letters for their name, sounding as you go. If her name is Sophia, pull out the "*S, ssssss.*" Then the "*o, ooooo.*" Next pull out the *p* and *h* together, "The *p* and *h* in your name go *fffffff.*" Lastly, pull out the *i* and *a*, "And the *i* and *a* in your name go together, like *iiiiaaa*. The *i* makes a special sound in your name because it's next to an *a*." (They don't need any fancy explanations at this point.) Point to each letter or letter combo as you pronounce, "*Ssss-ooo-fffff-iiiiaaa*. Sophia—that's your name!"
    - As you stack the dishes and prepare to wash them, create the word *dish* out of the magnets. "D-i-s-h … *dish*. The *s* and *h* together go *shhhh* for *dishhhh*." Show them how to put the letters in order from left to right to form the word.

- As they become familiar with structuring a word, have them find the letters and arrange them as you call them out. "Can you make the word *apple* as Mom cuts up an apple for our snack? *A...p...p...l...e – apple.*"
- There's no wrong way of choosing which letter case to use. In the beginning, I let them choose either case. This helped me see what they recognized. Usually they chose uppercase at first, then threw in lowercase as they began to recognize them. A word could look like this: *cLoCK*. That's ok. I had only begun to differentiate the cases and show them how to make them all one case(*clock*), or capitalize words(*Clock*) after they had a solid knowledge base for both cases.

FOOD FUN

- Expand on how you interacted with food for letters. Now build those letters into words (a pancake name, a simple word formed with their snack food—yum).
- After creating food letters, arrange the letters into words.
- Noodle Doodle: Form words (like with fridge magnets) out of cooked noodles.
- Eating Games: Have fun eating the words. Be dramatic and add emotion and inflection to make it fun and capture their interest.

- "*C-o-w...cow.* Let's eat the *c* first." Point to the remaining letters, "Oh-no! *Ow! Owwww!!* The cow is hurting because we ate its *c!* We should eat the *w* quick and see if that helps." Eat it, then moan, "*O. Oooooooo!* Uh-oh, whoops! I think my cow is dying. How about yours? We'd better put them out of their misery and eat the *o.*" Eat it, then give a big sigh of relief. "Whew, I'm glad those cows are quiet now. They sounded terrible!" Nine times out of ten they'll want to do this again with another "cow."

- This can also be done using actions. "*S-i-t...sit.* What should we eat first? The *t*? Ok." Eat the *t*, then stand up and exclaim, "Oh, no! We can't sit! We don't have a *t* anymore—*t-t-t.*" Act like you're trying to sit back down on the chair, but are not able to. With every attempt, grunt, "*si, si...*" After several attempts: "Now what should we do? Eat the *i*? Oh no, eat our *eyes?!*" Eat the *i*, covering one eye since it got eaten. "Oh, dear. We only have one eye now! What do we do?" Point to the *S*. "*Sssssss!* Hear that? A *ssssnake!* I'm a one-eyed snake! *Ssssss!* I'm gonna get you!" Amidst laughs and giggles, you pick up your *s* and "attack" each other with it, still holding a hand over one eye.

- Demonstrate how you can make a new word by rearranging the letters: "*P-i-t...pit.* Oh look! I can swap the *p* and *t*, and now it makes *t-i-p...tip.*"

- Show them how you can make new words after eating a letter. Make a sentence with each "new" remaining word, putting it in story form. Go ahead and make it silly. This helps them remember and engages their interest.
    - PITS→PIT→IT→I "This is the PITS!...Now there's just one peach PIT...What is IT?...It's an I—me! Oh, no, am *I* a peach pit?"
    - CATS→CAT→AT→A "I've got *100* CATS! Hmmm, now I only have one CAT...Where is my cat AT?...It went down to visit its friend, Miss A."
    - CHAIR→HAIR→AIR→AI→I "I'm sitting on my CHAIR...Oh, dear! There's a HAIR on my chair!...But look—the hair on my chair just floated into the AIR...*AI, ai, ai,* what happened to my *R?* (eat the *A*) Oh – I guess *I* ate it!"

MATCHING GAMES

- Match-a-Word
    - Use two decks of letter cards or the fridge magnets.
    - Create a word and have them copycat it.
    - Use uppercase, lowercase, then a combo to soft-test their skills.

LINKING LETTERS

- Word Search Puzzles: Your child doesn't have to be reading yet to successfully spot a letter-link. I would often work on word puzzles and invite my children to help me. If I was looking for the word repeat, they just needed to look for rc letters together. If the word was yellow, then spotting two l's usually broke the case. I'd show them how to verify that all the letters in the word lined up correctly. They loved "helping" me find words to my puzzles.

- Recognizing letter-links and learning to link letters takes your child another step forward in the process of learning to read.

- As with introducing many things: 1) start by asking for their help (gaining participation and interest), 2) invite them to try it, 3) before long, off they go, doing it on their own.

WHITEBOARD ACTIVITIES

- Word Jumble
    - Write a jumble of words on the board, each word in a different color.
    - Write one of the words above the jumble.
    - Have them point to, circle, or erase the word below that matches from the word jumble.

- Word Match
    - Write two columns containing the same set of words but in diffferent order. Have them draw lines matching the two columns.

ADVANCED WORK WITH WORDS

Whiteboard – Advanced Activities

- Point out a word they are learning while you write a note on the board.
- Write a word on the board. Have them sound it out.
- Read & Respond:
  - Write a word on the board *(Ex: the, of, and,* or a frequently used word in the book, i.e., *cat)*. Read a book and have them make a tally mark each time they hear the word in the story. They are both seeing the word and listening for it.
  - Write a bunch of words on the board from a storybook. Have them point to, circle, or erase each word as you read it from the book *(to, a, the,* as well as other words they are becoming familiar with).
  - To take it a step further, capitalize some of the words and they cannot erase them until a sentence starts with that word *(the, The)*. Use a different color for the capitalized words at first. This exercise helps them listen and identify the capitalized words. This will translate to improved capitalization when you get to that step in grammar.
- Letter Scramble:
  - Write three letters on the board and have them write a word with them. Show them how to identify the vowel first, then figure out on which side the other two letters go. *(igb: i…gib* or *big?)*

- Include some letter groups that make two words. Show them how to first make one word, then swap the letters around. *(apt: a...pat* and *tap)*
- As they advance, give them four letters to unscramble.

Games-on-the-Go

- Billboard & Sign (while driving)
    - Find words on billboards and signs while driving.
    - Find words starting with a certain letter, and more challenging, find words ending with a certain letter.
    - Find a word that begins with each letter of the alphabet (exception for *X:* find a word starting with *ex)*.
    - You can try it in alphabetical order or write down the alphabet and cross off letters when you see a word. You can do it individually or team up. You can do it as a race or as completion-for-a-prize.
    - Note: You can type up a Word doc with the letters and print off as needed. Include a line or space for older players to write down the words they find. Keep a stack in the vehicle for multiple players.
- Whiteboard Advanced Activities "on-the-go"
    - After introducing the concepts and activities on the whiteboard (see above section), you can use them whenever you have time to pass or need a quiet activity (church, waiting room, road trip, etc.).

- Words-Within-a-Word
    - Write down a nice long word (or two), preferably one that they will enjoy. *(hippopotamus, beautiful, quarterback, hayrack ride, swimming pool)*
    - Have them find as many words as they can using those letters. *(hippopotamus = hip, pot, top, hop, pop, pup, sum, hum, map, hot, moo...)*
    - As they get older, see if they can find some 4-letter words. *(stop, hoop, shut, soap, pump, moat, atom, auto, path, past, push...)*
    - You can also play it with your child, requiring 5+ words from yourself. *(photo, opium, utopia, thump, stamp, south, spout, autism, hiatus, utmost, pompous, shampoo...)*

HANDWRITING & EARLY GRAMMAR

TIPS:

- Begin practicing handwriting on larger surfaces using larger tools than the standard pen/pencil and 8.5x11 paper.
- Besides the whiteboard, more fun options are finger paint, paintbrushes, gel pens, markers, a roll of paper, and outside in the dirt or sand with a stick or their fingers.
- Start with uppercase letters and then introduce the lowercase.
- Encourage them to start out by writing slowly. Good form needs to come first. The temptation is to start writing at quicker speeds before having mastered the motor skill and muscle memory to do so.

PRINTING LETTERS

See Chapter 8—Wonders of the Whiteboard, under "Writing at the Whiteboard"

- Start with the whiteboard.
- Practice with paint and markers.
- Together, draw letters outside in the dirt or sand.
- Don't worry about the size of a letter at this point.
- Say a letter and have them write it.

PRACTICAL TIPS & IDEAS

Letter Practice

- Sensory-Letters
  - Fill the bottom of a baking pan with sugar, sand, or shaving cream.
  - Have your child trace letters in it.
- Letter Matching—practicing with cases
  - Write a lowercase letter, have them write the uppercase letter.
  - Then write uppercase letters and have them write lowercase letters.
  - Mix up the practice with both uppercase and lowercase.
  - Demonstrate that a gigantic *a* is still a lowercase *a*, and a tiny *A* is still an uppercase *A*. It has nothing to do with size, but its shape.
- Vowel Recognition
  - Write out the alphabet together using a different color for the vowels.
  - Write a mixture of vowels and consonants at the top and have them write out only the vowels.
- Letter Scramble
  - Write a jumble of letters at the top of the board and have them write the letters in alphabetical order as you sing the alphabet song together. (*g, e, i, s, d, z, p, a* = *a, d, e, g, i, p, s, z*)

- Write out varying multiples of a set of letters and have them write out one of each letter. They can cross off the extra letters as they write them out. (five *w's*, four *h's*, four *c's*, three *x's*, two *j's*, and one *m* = *w, h, c, x, j, m*)

Introducing Correct Size and Slant

- Make large dotted ruled lines with wet-erase markers. Then draw one solid-lined practice letter and a couple dotted-lined practice letters. Have them practice with dry-erase markers on the white board.
    - Staying within the lines
    - All lines straight (d not *d*)
- When they are ready, transition them to a pencil with the pre-printed handwriting practice paper. (You can make it yourself with wide-ruled notepad paper. Make the lines with a heavier pen, like a fine-edged marker.) Draw the solid and dotted-lined practice letters in pen. A colored pen helps it stand out from the lines a little better and makes it easier for them to follow.

PRINTING WORDS

Letter Spacing

- Overexaggerate incorrect spacing with a longer name or word they are familiar with. Point out how the letters do not look connected like the words in a book do. Get out a book and show them how all the letters to each word are grouped together evenly.
    - *M a r ian n a*

- Explain how all the letters in one word must be closer together than the spaces between the words. Demonstrate how impossible it would be to read if the letters were not spaced properly into their intended words. Incorrectly write a sentence that they could normally read:
  - T hem an r a na f t ert h ec a t.
- Demonstrate how difficult it is to read those letters. Try sounding out the "words" to read the sentence together…it won't work and will sound weird. Now underneath, rewrite the sentence correctly and show them the huge difference it makes.
  - The man ran after the cat.
- Point: it is important to have the same amount of space between each letter, with about double the space between each word.
- Let them practice.
  - Start with two- and three-letter words.
  - Continue to simple short sentences.

CURSIVE HANDWRITING

Follow the concepts of teaching printed letters.

- Start at the whiteboard with large dotted ruled lines made with wet erase markers, and practice with dry-erase markers.
- Again, draw one solid-lined practice letter, then a couple dotted-lined practice letters.

- Follow the same procedure to transition them to a pencil with the handwriting practice paper. Again, draw the solid and dotted-lined practice letters for them in colored pen.
- Refresh their understanding about letter and word spacing.

The Slant Difference

- The biggest difference between printed and cursive letters (besides the weird way some of the letters are shaped) is the angle of the letters.
    - Printed is vertical.
    - Cursive is *slanted.*
- Helpful hints for slanting letters:
    - Tip the paper slightly more to the left (rotating the paper slightly counterclockwise).
    - The amount you tip your paper will result in the increased or decreased angle of the letters.
    - You can test this by angling the paper different degrees and writing the same way you always do. Your child needs to become familiar with the new angle required for properly slanted cursive writing. Help them angle their paper until it becomes more automatic for them.

Note: Slant has more to do with the overall look of "messy" or "nice" than the actual shape the letters have.

- Demonstrate this by writing well shaped letters, but mixing up the slants:
  - Write some forward slanting, some straight, and some backwards slanting, all in varying measures.
  - Take a pen and draw a vertical line through the letter, showing its angle.
- Then do the opposite:
  - Keep all letters *slanting* forward, but don't form them perfectly.
  - Again, take a pen and draw a vertical line through the letter, showing their (hopefully) symmetric angle.
- Review both styles.
- Show your child that even if he writes the letter correctly, if he is not careful about the slant, it can still appear messy.
- To refine handwriting, focus on both:
  - Nicely formed letters PLUS:
  - A little slant forward (not too much, nor slanting backwards).

SPELLING & VOCABULARY

SPECTACULAR SPELLING

The Dictionary

To my dismay, one of my mom's favorite lines to spelling or definition questions was, "Look it up in the dictionary!" It was one of those things I thought I'd never do to my kids…until I began to realize what a valuable tool it was. To my children's chagrin, it also became one of my favorite lines as well. Though the paperback was what was available to me, and mostly with my children, the online dictionary is now a great resource as well.

- Stimulates self-learning.
- Enhances alphabetical order skills.
- Improves dictionary skills.
- Enlarges vocabulary.
- The Dictionary Game
    - Player 1 chooses an unknown word from the dictionary and writes it down for all players to see.
    - Without letting anyone see, Player 1 writes down the correct answer on a slip of paper.
    - All other players write down a creative answer on a separate slip of paper.
    - All answers are given face-down to Player 1.

- Player 1 reads the answers, including the correct one. Each player guesses the right answer.
- Each player who guessed the right answer gets a point. Each player who had their answer creation guessed gets a point. And if no one gets the right answer, Player 1 gets three points.

Spelling Activities

- Make a fun crossword puzzle.
- Do word search puzzles.
- Create word puzzles online and print them off.
- Create rhymes and poems together.

Spelling Games

- Rhyme-a-Word Game
    - First person says a word. Next person has to say a word that rhymes, or they're "out." Play goes on until there's only one player left. Can be played with just two people… first one who can't rhyme loses.
- Category Game
    - Determine a category. Take turns saying a word from that category. Players are "out" if they cannot think of a word.
    - Make this more restrictive by limiting answers to beginning with a certain letter. (category = vegetables, letter = B)
    - Increase the difficulty by adding a time limit for answers.

SPELLING & VOCABULARY

- Words-Within-a-Word
    - Hippopotamus example.
    - Details listed earlier in the Phonics & Reading section under "Advanced Work with Words."
    - Try for 4-5 letter words.
    - Put a timer on. See how many words each person can list before the timer goes off.
- Make-a-Code
    - Label the alphabet with numbers, colors, and symbols.
    - Create a message with the new substitutions.
    - Give the labeled alphabet sheet and the message to Dad when he gets home and see if he can crack the code!
- Fast-Scrabble
    - Using only the tiles, lay them face down on the table.
    - Each player starts with 7 tiles.
    - Each player creates their own personal "Scrabble" puzzle using the 7 letters.
    - Each time someone uses up all their letters, they call out, "Draw 2!"
    - Draw and add these letters to existing words, or disassemble and rearrange the letters into new words.
    - The game continues until the tiles are gone and the first person to finish using up all their tiles is the winner.

- Bag-of-Nouns
    - Played in teams, minimum of four players.
    - Without the others seeing, each player writes out five nouns on separate squares of paper, folds them, and places them in a brown lunch bag.
    - A timer gets set for one minute. Game is played in three rounds.
    - Round 1: Player 1 reaches into the bag, pulls out a noun, and describes it without using the word (like Taboo). He finishes as many words as he can before the timer goes off. Team 1 gets one point per word guessed correctly. All words are returned to the bag. Play cycles until each player has had one turn.
    - Round 2: This time Player 1 must get his teammates to guess each noun by saying only ONE word. (It helps to recall the noun names from the previous round.) If a player says more than one word, they forfeit the remainder of their time, and the points are tallied up.
    - Round 3: The last round is played like Charades or Guesstures, with no words allowed, only actions. At the end of the round, the team with the most points wins.

Spelling Bees

- Host a Spelling Bee at supper. Give age appropriate words to each family member.
- Everyone can play:
  - Write out several words for each person.
  - Cut the words apart, fold the papers, and place them in a bowl. Label each bowl for each person.
  - Going around the circle, take turns picking a word for the next person and checking their spelling. All older siblings can read the younger children's words, and Dad and Mom get to read each other their words.
  - Keep score on the whiteboard.
  - Variation: play teams.

SPELLING WORD ACTIVITIES

Easy

- Trace over words using colored pens.
- Draw a picture for each word.
- Cut out letters from newspaper and magazines to make words.
- Write words with sidewalk chalk.
- Spell words aloud in rhythm with an exercise, like jumping jacks.
- Use uncooked alphabet pasta or Scrabble tiles to spell words.

Intermediate

- Rhyme each word.
- Find each word in the dictionary and read the definitions.
- Write a sentence with each word.
- Type words in different colors, fonts, and sizes.
- Add-It-Up
    - Vowels are 10 cents and consonants are 5 cents.
    - Calculate the value of each word.
- Play the Memory game.
    - Write words out twice and cut apart.
    - Mix them, place face down and then make matches.
    - Can play with multiple players. Even the younger siblings may be able to recognize some letter layouts and find a match, especially with easier words.

Advanced

- Write words in alphabetical order, forward and backwards.
- Write words in order of how many letters they contain.
- Sort words grammatically: (nouns, verbs, adjectives, etc.).
- Clap out the syllables. Write words in columns according to the number of syllables they contain (Can also divide the words into syllables).
- Write a synonym and antonym for each word.

BOOSTING VOCABULARY

Make a habit of adding new words regularly into your child's vocabulary "toolbox."

- Read, read, read, read…
    - Books, magazines, billboards, directions, etc.
    - Read to them, even as they get older and can read for themselves.
    - Read a larger, full-sized book as a family on a road trip, before bed, etc.
- Introduce words beyond their comprehension level. Games like Balderdash or "The Dictionary Game" are good for this.
    - Learn a new word a week.
    - Practice using it applicably.
    - *Sty: a pigpen.* "Your room needs to be cleaned up. It looks like a sty."
- Use a thesaurus to look up synonyms to known words.
    - This will help expand your word base and be more creative in describing things.
    - Thesaurus.com is an excellent resource.
    - Make a list of familiar words. Use a thesaurus to write out a list of new words. Practice using the new words and put a reward system in place for when a new word is used correctly.

- Reports and Typing Skills
    - Introduce the concept of reports by having them give short oral reports on a book they just read.
    - As printing is established, have them print their report.
    - As handwriting is demonstrated, have them write their reports in cursive.
    - As writing is achieved, have them type up the report.

THE LIBRARY AND INTERNET

The library is a great resource for books, research, music, videos, and free internet usage. Often, they have special rooms available for studying or watching videos.

- Go to the library to specifically look up and search for something with your child, teaching them in action how your library operates.
- Use the library to teach and learn the Dewey decimal system and your library's organizational system.
- Check out books as you learn about topics for school.
- Check out music CDs of famous classical artists like Bach and Beethoven to play during school or quiet time.
- Use educational videos that support and supplement your subjects or give good advice and information.

The Internet

- One of your greatest suppliers for up-to-date information, teaching tools, and how-to videos, is the internet.
    - Model and teach your children healthy online boundaries and hygiene.
    - Teach them how to search, research, and type proficiently.
- Open a Google account.
    - Google Drive is an easy place to create, save, and store documents, photos, and more.
    - Have your child work with the different tools that Google offers.
- Type up reports and papers using a document template.
- Create a spreadsheet for a personal budget, chore list, or school schedule.
- Put a presentation together on a country or science item you've learned about.
- Create a questionnaire or survey and then have them make a graph with the information collected.
- Use the drawing tool to play around with and get familiar with graphics.
- Compose an email to practice composition and typing skills. Send the email to grandparents, family, or friends. If you prefer to keep the emails within your family initially, for practice, address them to yourself, having your children send replies and responses back and forth to each other.

VERBAL & SPEECH SKILLS

Sharing around the supper table offers practice in speech and delivery skills, and it gives the "audience" a chance to practice active listening skills. It also gives the "speaker" special-attention time, especially when Dad is present. They can each take a turn sharing, and each have a night that they present something to the family.

This is a great way to put into practice voice inflection, speaking with confidence, and making what they are reading interesting to others. After the speaker has "presented," invite the audience to respond by asking questions or making comments about the presentation. What did they like or didn't like? What did they understand or didn't understand?

Encouraging comments encourages active listening. Before the speaker begins, you can let everyone know that afterwards you want to hear one thing they liked about what the speaker talked about. They will need to pay attention in order to participate.

Voice Inflection

To avoid monotone reading, demonstrate how to read according to how the punctuation marks dictate. This will benefit and strengthen their ability to read out loud.

- Comma = a pause
- Semi-colon = a longer pause
- End of sentence = the longest pause

- Period = ending the sentence with a voice inflection downward, just like you do when you talk.
- Exclamation point = ending the sentence with a voice inflection upward.
- Question mark = ending the sentence with a voice inflection "squiggly." Like a "~" mark, the tone goes up, down, then up again in a questioning manner.

"Public" Speaking

- Telling about a picture they drew or colored.
- Sharing a new concept they learned in a subject.
- Reading a paper they wrote.
- Reading a poem from their literature book.
- Reciting a poem they memorized.
- Reading from the Bible.
- Reciting a Bible verse they memorized.
- Telling about something they learned that day.
- Sharing something about their day that was meaningful to them.
- Sharing something that reminded them about God that day.

MATHEMATICS

TIPS

- ✏ Just like your child must know to count before completing a dot-to-dot puzzle, teaching math in daily life before teaching it on paper helps your child to connect those dots as well.
- ✏ Learning math with life application is powerful and memorable.
- ✏ Use the whiteboard to demonstrate and have your child practice.
- ✏ When introducing a new topic on paper, especially scarier things like fractions, decimals, and percentages, it helps to assure your child that they already know the content—that now they are just learning what it looks like on paper.
- ✏ Remember to make it as fun or enjoyable as possible.

THE TIMER

Teaching children the value of a minute is very useful and serves as a great motivator, for both home life and school times. Good ways to teach the idea of time are through physical activity, enforced inactivity, for competition, and while making an observation. They gain an appreciation for the measure of time.

- Time them as they run outside—around the house, around the yard, around the block, etc.
- Do jumping jacks for a minute, or two, or five.

- Count with the timer, either counting up or counting down.
- See if they can finish a task before the timer goes off: putting away the dishes or their clothes, feeding the dog, etc.
- Time how quickly they can do things like tie their shoes, get the mail, say their ABC's, count pennies, etc.
- Time how long they can hold their breath—there are health benefits to this!
- Time how long they can perform a wall sit (sitting against a wall with knees and hips at 90 degrees each). This is a great exercise to expend energy in the house when it's bad weather outside.
- Put a timer on for quiet time, taking a bath, playing on electronics, etc.
- Time how long it takes for an egg to cook.
- Let them hold the timer for beating pudding for two minutes—or have them do the beating.
- As they get older, time their flash cards and some quick tests. See Chapter 10—Personalized Curriculum, Grading, & Testing, under "Personalized 'Hard' Testing."

TELLING TIME

A fun way to transition from the appreciation of time to the reading of time (on a clock) is to affix numbers clock-style on the floor and have them "walk the clock." Set up your "clock" in a larger area, like a living room rug or a basement area. You can use colored tape for the numbers, or tape down paper with the numbers written or drawn on them.

PRACTICAL TIPS & IDEAS

WALKING THE CLOCK

- Walk in step (or march) together around the clock, counting as you go. Emphasize the fives: "1, 2, 3, 4, *5*... 6, 7, 8, 9, *10*..."
- Take "giant steps" or hop from number to number as you call out the fives: "*5, 10, 15, 20*..." As they learn their fives, have them count with you.
- Stand beside a number as they walk around the clock. (example: 10) Call out and count that specific hour's time: "10:*05*, 10:*10*, 10:*15*, 10:*20*..."
- Be the "hour hand," stand on a number (example: 2), and call out a time. Have them stand where the minute hand would be pointing: "2:15"…they go stand on the 3. "2:55"…they go stand on the *11*.
- Swap and have them be the "hour hand" and call out a time. Have them check that you stepped on the correct number.
- If you want to emphasize the half-hours, highlight the *6* and *12* in a different color. When you want to focus on the quarter-hours, add highlights to the *3* and *9* as well. Or, if you want to practice counting by *10*'s, highlight *2, 4, 6, 8, 10, 12*.

You can introduce initial counting by *5's, 10's,* and *15's* using a floor clock like this. Then, you can make a reusable practice clock with a paper or plastic plate. Write or paint the numbers around the edge and use a brad paper fastener to connect cutouts of an hour hand and a minute hand. Affix the minute hand on top of the hour hand. With this clock you can do further practice with time and counting. Later when you introduce Roman numerals, you can make a new clock to practice with.

LEARNING FRACTIONS IN THE KITCHEN

Introducing fractions through cooking and baking is super easy. Start feeding them the love for being in the kitchen with you as soon as they can sit on the counter (or pull up the high chair for them to watch). Let them observe you. Before long, they will want to help. Let them. It's an investment. It will be messier, stickier, and more time-consuming, but worth it.

I go in-depth with more details and tips in Chapter 9—Practice with Everyday Learning, under "Practice in Real Life" and in Chapter 10—Personalized Curriculum, Grading, & Testing, under "Soft Testing Without Anxiety."

- As you hand them a teaspoon of baking powder or a cup of flour to dump in the bowl, name aloud what you're giving them: "a cup of flour," "a fourth teaspoon of salt," etc.
- Give a running commentary about what you're doing and why. It doesn't matter that they can't yet understand everything—they love that you are including them.
- It will become natural for you to refer to cup, teaspoon, and tablespoon measurements. As they get a little older, they will pick up the kitchen lingo, which is perfect for transferring their knowledge to school.
- Use water to understand measurement conversion: cups, pints, quarts, and gallons. On a hot summer day, take this outside for some wet 'n' wild water fun.
- Add fractions by doubling a recipe with them.
- Multiply and divide fractions by multiplying a recipe three times or cutting one in half or thirds.

- To understand easy adding of fractions, use water to demonstrate the total of differing amounts of measurements. Examples:
    - ½ c + ½ c = 1 c
    - ¾ c + ¼ c = 1 c,
    - three ⅓ c = 1 c
    - four ¼ teaspoons = 1 t
    - two ¼ t = ½ t

I would grade written work in fraction form (+7/10), emphasizing how many they got correct. In this way, I was also using fractions in a way that was meaningful to them. Later I would be able to teach them how to divide these grades into percentages. I give the details of this in Chapter 10—Personalized Curriculum, Grades, & Testing, under "Letter Grades vs. True Understanding."

PRACTICAL MATH MEASUREMENTS

Be aware of measurement-related things you can point out and ask questions about in your home, on the road, and in your vehicle. Point out, demonstrate, and practice. Be purposeful in including them in the math process, no matter how minor, and give a short explanation about what you're doing and why.

- Use a ruler to make a paper project.
- Use a yardstick to measure your child's height (don't use a measuring tape when you can include some mental math by adding the 36 inches plus the remainder for the total; have them help you with the math).

- Use a measuring tape to move furniture, see if it will fit through a doorway or work well in a specific spot.
- Measure the miles to places as you drive short and long distances.
- Talk about mph and help connect the dots between 60 mph to being one mile per minute. Have them guesstimate the time for road trips.
- Measure tenths of a mile as you go down a long lane, how long it is around a town block, etc. (later show that tenths are decimals and that they already are familiar with them).
- Practice adding decimals in a practical way while on a trip by adding up the mileage shown on maps.

VOLUME

A simple and easy way to introduce the vocabulary, concepts, and understanding of volume is by eyeballing leftovers and choosing a container to put it away in. Or moving contents of an open package into something airtight.

My daughter and I made a game out of it and still enjoy occasionally competing after a meal. We'll call out the size of container that we calculate will be the closest fit for our food remnant. Then, we fill our containers and compare. My daughter is a worthy and formidable opponent.

Sometimes we guessed the volume perfectly and scored. Other times we undercalculated and had to finish with an additional container. Sometimes we overcalculated and needed to switch to a smaller container to keep the food fresh and lessen the oxidation from exposure to air. Early on, I had explained the need for the food to fit the container without a lot of extra air—thus adding science to the mix.

ANGLES IN APPLICATION

Angles involve every shape imaginable, from a straight line to a circle. From points and lines to arcs and degrees. This makes it easy to point out and introduce into your child's vocabulary. Below are a few examples to get your creative juices flowing.

- 360 degrees (a circle):
    - Draw circles or have the child point out round things like a clock, a plate, a penny, the sun, a wheel, a smiley face.
    - Add a verse to the famous song, and sing, "the wheels on the bus are three-six-ty, three-six-ty, three-six-ty…"
- 180 degrees (a straight line):
    - Hanging a picture. Simply include the verbiage at the teachable moment as you demonstrate how to use a level to hang a picture straight. "We want to make sure this is straight at a 180-degree angle, parallel with this other picture."
    - In giving directions. Use sentences and insert "180 degrees" with the concept of "straight ahead." The point is also being made for "no dillydallying," that you want the job done without distractions: "What you're looking for is a straight 180 degrees in front of you." Adding rhyme: "Run straight down the drive 180 *degrees* and return with the mail, *please*."
- 90 degrees (a right angle)
    - Teaching good sitting posture (you can include a quick biology lesson). Demonstrate it while saying in a sing-songy voice, "Hips and knees at 90 degrees…it's the *right*

way to sit!" Then when you introduce right angles in the book, just ask them, "What is the *right* way to sit?"

- o You can also draw a stick figure on the whiteboard, pointing out the right angles. Make a circle, then draw a line downward, to the right, and downward again in equal proportions. As you create the 90-degree angles of the hips and knees, put emphasis to your words as you repeat, "Hips and knees at 90 degrees…it's the *right* way to sit!"

- Acute and Obtuse Angles: smaller and larger than 90-degree angles. These angles are fun being demonstrated with your arms.
  - o Acute: Position your arms like they are arms on a clock for 3 o'clock. Ask, "Is it acute or obtuse?" Bring your right arm up to create 1 o'clock. Answer in a way you'd exclaim over a baby, "Awww, it's "*a-cute*" little angle!" as you emphasize that "acute" is less than 90 degrees.
  - o Obtuse: Again, position your arms at 3 o'clock and ask, "Is it acute or obtuse?" Drop your left arm outward toward the "10" position. Announce in a sing-songy voice, "Ob-tuse: hang loose!" You'll be showing them how an obtuse angle is greater than 90 degrees but not all the way to a 180-degree straight line.
  - o Randomly ask what kind of angle something is. Wonder out loud what type of angle something might be. "Is this a right angle, or is it acute or obtuse?" If they're not sure, it gives you the opportunity to demonstrate your arm movements again. If they answer you immediately, ask them why. Have them "prove" their answer by using the corresponding arm movements.

GEOMETRY

I loved to point out everywhere I saw geometry. The arrangement and symmetry of shapes, lines, and points. We are surrounded by them. I called this "applied geometry." From very young, my children were familiar with the term geometry. And no, it was not the sentence, "Gee, Ah'm a tree!"

Now, my kids can't resist commenting on something geometrical or congratulating themselves on a job well done. "Look at that applied geometry, Mom! Isn't it fantastic?" Of course, from the boys, it sounds more like, "Oh, hey Mom, check out this applied geometry." I love that they have come to recognize and appreciate the beauty of geometry in their life.

Point out the geometry as you notice, recognize, or are demonstrating it:

- Putting games away on a shelf.
- Stacking boxes in a storage room or shed.
- Loading a vehicle for vacation.
- Putting groceries into a box or paper bag.
- Layering bars or cheese slices onto a platter.
- Lining up dominoes, building with them or creating a design.
- Basically anything that involves shapes to create a pattern or is Tetris-like, by making the most out of the space available.

MONEY

Money is a great way to teach many things in math. A child generally catches onto the value of money at an early age, making it perfect to use. You can help establish the value of money with awards, wages, allowances, consequences, and purchases.

WORKING WITH MONEY

Once your child has a greater understanding of the value of money, you can use it in other ways as well. Using allowances and consequences are a great way to build work ethic and improve money management. It can be done in different ways. Tweak a style that suits you, your children, and your schedule.

- One way is to give them credit on the front end of the week. If they need a visual, place the money in a glass jar.
- Have a consequence list with monetary value attached. This can include whatever is appropriate or what you are working on at the time. Anything from attitude and obedience to quality of work and remembering chores without a reminder.
- As they pay for a consequence, remove the coins. At the end of the week, they get to keep whatever is in their jar. You can also add opportunities and odd jobs to earn money to compensate for the losses from the consequences.
- As you progress to math on paper, you can keep a notebook next to the jar and keep a running tally.
- When learning simple math, let them add or subtract each entry. As they get older, have them learn to use a calculator at the end of the week to verify accuracy.

INTRODUCING FRACTIONS, DECIMALS, & PERCENTAGES

After introducing fractions in recipes for cooking and baking, they will get practice writing out fractions if you have them help you double or divide a recipe. Just this exercise will prepare them for further work with fractions on paper later.

Early decimal work is best introduced with money. You don't necessarily have to use the term "decimal." So long as your child is familiar with money—can count it, add it, subtract it, and knows how to write it out properly, i.e. "$3.25"—they are prepared to learn about the concept of decimals on paper.

Percentages can seem overwhelming to teach. However, they are actually really easy to introduce, and to transfer that understanding to paper. You are already using percentage phrases in your daily language with store sales, like "25% off." You are likely also using electronics and speaking percentage terms in regard to their battery life. These two areas alone are enough to introduce your child to the concept of percentages.

Fractions, decimals, and percentages are all different ways to express the same amount of a number or the same part of the whole. They say the same thing three different ways, and we use them to express math in different ways in life.

$$\tfrac{1}{2} = .50 = 50\%$$

FRACTIONS TO DECIMALS - CONCEPT OF CONVERSION

Before introducing decimals on paper, my children knew the value of "$3.25." They understood that dollars were on the left side of the dot and cents were on the right side. They knew mental math, that 3.25 and 3.25

was 6.50 because 3+3=6 and .25 + .25 = .50. I would start by showing my children the connection between fractions and decimals.

The easiest way is to use money and measuring cups. Get out the quarters, dimes, nickels, and a dollar bill. Also collect the ¼, ½, ¾, and 1 cup measurements. (Although you can use "one-quarter" and "one-fourth" interchangeably, I am using ¼ as "one-fourth.")

First with Hands-On

- Place the ¼ cup next to a quarter and explain that one-quarter and one-fourth is the same, whether the term is used for money or ingredients.
    - Each one indicates one of four parts. The fourth part of a dollar or the fourth part of a cup.
    - Point out that "the quarter's name even says that it is a quarter of a dollar!"
- Take four quarters. Placing one quarter beside the dollar bill = "one-quarter of a dollar."
    - Lay the second quarter next to the first quarter = "two-quarters, or two is half of four, so half of a dollar."
    - Lay down the third quarter = "three-quarters of a dollar."
    - Lay the final quarter down = "one full dollar." The dollar bill adds visual connection to this exercise.
- Connect the quarters with the measuring cups. Explain as you do this: place one quarter (representative of ¼ c water) into the ¼ cup, then dump it into the 1 cup measurement.
    - Repeat three times until you "fill" the cup. Then, reverse the process and empty the cup.

PRACTICAL TIPS & IDEAS

- - Mix it up by placing one quarter in the ¼ cup, three quarters in the ¾ cup, and placing the dollar bill inside the 1 cup measurement. They will follow these connections.
- Without using paper yet, just get them familiar with using the verbiage and practicing orally while they manipulate coins around.
  - You can use dimes and nickels for practice with additional coins.
  - They'll catch on that 25 cents is 25 cents, regardless of which coin(s) are being used.

Soft Testing

- Give them a pre-counted pile of coins and ask them for ¼, ½, or ¾ of them.
- Branch out from money and ingredients.
  - Begin with easy questions like, "If there were 100 people in the room, and 25 people left, what is the fraction of those that left?
  - What fraction stayed?
  - How would you write that as a decimal?"
- Progress to scenarios like, "I give you twelve jelly beans. You share four with your sister and four with your brother."
  - "What fraction did you keep for yourself?"
  - "What fraction did you share?"
  - "What fraction did each of you eat?"
  - "How do you write those as decimals?"

MATHEMATICS

- You can also use small food items like peanuts in real time.
  - Count out eight peanuts, "You may eat ¼ of this pile."
  - After he's eaten two, "Now give ½ of this pile to your brother."
  - With the three left, "Please give ⅔ of this pile to me."
  - After you eat two, "Now you may eat the last one."

Beginning on Paper

- With the money and measuring cups right there, grab a piece of blank paper.
- Show them that $.25 is ¼, $.50 is ½, and $.75 is ¾.
  - It's super easy as you refer to the four quarters and measuring cups which they are already familiar with.
  - Then reverse it and show how to write ¼, ½, and ¾ as decimals: .25, .50, and .75.
  - Do some quick and easy practice mixing it up in both directions.
- You can even have them "test" you. Sometimes this can be very effective.
  - They play "teacher," write out the different forms of fractions and decimals, and then you take the test and get some right and some wrong.
  - They grade and write your grade at the top in fraction form, like +8/10. The goal is for them to grade accurately.
- Another fun way is to include some of the youngsters.
  - Have your "teacher" make a matching test for them. They must include all four forms they've learned in each column.

- The younger child(ren) have fun drawing lines between the two columns.
- Then, they turn the paper back in to the "teacher" for grading. The siblings get practice drawing lines, and the "teacher" gets additional grading practice.

• Do simple adding and subtracting with the fractions and decimals. Things they already know in their heads and verbally, they now are putting on paper.
  - ¼ + ½ = ¾
  - ⅔ - ⅓ = ⅓
  - .75 - .25 = .50
  - .50 + .50 = 1 (same as $1.00)

Converting the Thirds

• Since thirds are not an even number, you can skip it initially or teach it on another lesson. The best way I've found to demonstrate thirds with money or as a decimal is to have them divide up 100 pennies into three piles.

• With the leftover penny, explain that since we cannot cut it into thirds, we just write .33 and .66, which equals .99. This will suffice initially until you go into the division for it later.

FRACTIONS TO DECIMALS AND BEYOND – DIVISION WORK ON PAPER

I start with a whiteboard. If you use paper, blank is best. The brain needs to concentrate on the numbers instead of being distracted by the lines on ruled pages. They will need to know division.

- The immediate great news to tell your child is that learning how to convert a fraction to a decimal on paper requires learning nothing new. They are just learning how to show the conversion calculations on paper. It's only a matter of division, which they already know.
- A fraction problem is really just a division problem written in a different way:
    - ¼ can also be said, "1 divided by 4." Simple.
    - Demonstrate by using the example of converting ¼ to a decimal.
    - Write out and solve the short division problem.
- The answer (.25) is the decimal value of the fraction (¼).
    - This gives you a reference point and helps them understand the process.
    - It also helps them apply the calculations to any fraction.
    - Next do a few more easy practice fractions that they already know the answer to, like ½ and ¾.
- Once they're getting the hang of it, pull out one of their textbooks.
    - Point out a fraction grade you've written and let them know that +17/20 can also be expressed as "17 divided by 20."
    - Write out the division problem and solve it with them: .85.
- From here, it's an easy next step to percentages:
    - Point out that by simply moving the decimal point over two places and adding a percent sign, their grade is 85%.

- - That's all it takes to convert decimals to percentages. It's so easy!
  - Now start going through some of their past grades and convert them to percentage grades.
  - Keep the work meaningful and relevant.
- This is when I explain how ⅓ is .33, divided and rounded down.
- If they ever get stuck, the best tip is to remind them how to convert ¼ to .25. By remembering that process, they can correctly convert any fraction into a decimal.

PROGRESSING TO PERCENTAGES

After gaining a good grasp on fraction and decimal conversions, adding percentages to the mix is super easy. If you introduced the initial concept of percentages like I did above, then they already know that percentages are nothing to be afraid of.

Your cell phone battery is another good place to continue the explanation. It is perfect to incorporate the concept of percentage.

Fractions and Percentages

- Show them your battery icon and ask, "How much of my battery would be left if it was showing 50%?"
  - Their likely answer will be "a half." Right.
  - "And how do we write out a half?"
  - This intro will connect the dots between percentages and fractions.

Decimals and Percentage

- Next, it's an easy step to include the decimals.
    - Refer back to money if necessary.
    - "So, if 50% is ½, remember how we write ½ as a decimal?" (what is ½ of a dollar?)
- Review the conversion process between decimals and percentages.
    - It is only about moving the decimal point two places.
    - To the right for a percentage, to the left for a decimal.
    - Use their grades as a reference point to remember the correct direction.

Easy Fluidity Among the Three

- Review how ½ and .50 are the same, and show how 50% is also the same.
- They all describe the same amount of food, money, or answer on the paper.
- The quickest example is to use 50 cents.
    - "This is $.50, or ½ of a dollar, or 50% of a dollar."
    - To frame it in a different way, fill a glass half full. "The glass is ½ full. The glass is .50 full. The glass is 50% full."
    - No matter which answer is used, it is correct.
- Next, do this on paper.
    - Either with a visual or a drawing, have them write out all three ways to answer for 25% and 75%.

MATH IN PUBLIC

When I went shopping for clothes, I loved to shop the sales for good deals. The kids and I would figure out how much an item was. It was more fun in stores because I let them to use the calculator.

I would also have the kids take turns keeping track of the price of each item as I put it in my grocery cart. When we checked out, we'd check their sum against the receipt before tax. As they got older and were able to compute the tax, it was a challenge to see how close they got to the total.

When we went out to eat, I walked the kids through mental math for the tip. I did not want them to become overly dependent on a calculator. I taught them my 3-Step Rule.

The 3-Step Rule for Tipping

- Step 1: Figure out 10% of the total bill.
    - Take total and move decimal one point to the left.
    - A total of $43.80 is $4.38.
- Step 2: Round up for easy math. $4.38 = $4.50
- Step 3: Double that number for 20%. $4.50 = $9.00

I recommend modeling generosity with your tip. If you can't afford to tip at least 20%, don't go out to eat. In this example, we would tip $10.00. We love tipping generously in order to bless. If we were going out on a limited budget, we would calculate ahead of time what we could spend in order to have plenty left over for our tip.

FINANCES & STEWARDSHIP

TIPS

- These areas are built upon the foundations of integrity and honesty, and are taught using moral and biblical principles.
- The Bible mentions money over 800 times. The way we handle it is important to God and affects our character.
- What you teach and allow your child to do at younger ages will be more likely to stick with them as they get older. Waiting until later to begin teaching these principles can result in their rejection of them.
- Do not be guilty of, "Do as I say, not as I do." It will never work. Children will always follow what you do, even if they show temporary outward compliance of doing what you say.
- You will learn a lot about your children (and yourself) through interactions about money and money management.

HEALTHY FINANCES

We value what we save for and what we have paid for. I wanted my children to learn fiscal responsibility and be good stewards of their money and wise with their finances. I wanted to teach them the basics of giving, spending, saving, and debt while they were young.

I wanted them to be familiar with real-world finances, not live in a financial fantasy world for a large chunk of their childhood and then be unprepared for real life decisions and consequences. My goal was to imitate the principles and concepts of real-life money management into their young world of understanding.

BE A CHEERFUL GIVER

Giving satisfies a deep need within us and is more rewarding than most of us realize. We were created in our Maker's image, and He is a generous and gracious giver.

We taught our children about tithe and offering from a young age. They learned about the special blessing of the tithe and how tithing is a way to honor God and the increase He has given. According to Malachi 3:8-12, not tithing is equivalent to stealing from God. He invites us to test Him and His faithfulness toward us for provision.

The tithe tests our hearts. Are we dependent on our money or God for provision? And it is to be given with a cheerful heart, not with reluctance. We taught our children these principles and they grew up excited to give.

They understood that the first 10% belongs to God, and that additional offerings to a person or ministry are investments into the kingdom of God. This is how to store up treasure in heaven where nothing can corrupt. As a result, they can experience the blessings of God's banking and provision in their life.

I wanted my children to be giving-focused rather than receiving-focused in other areas as well. When our children were as young as three years old, we would give them money to buy Christmas gifts for us parents and their siblings. I'd give them $1.00 plus tax per gift. Then we went to a dollar store where we split up to help them shop. Sometimes an aunt or friend came along to help.

We made this a special outing that became a family tradition. After several years, I had the kids use their own money. We kept the amount at $1.00 until the children decided they wanted to increase the amount. They experienced the truth that it is more blessed to give than to receive.

To this day, we still all buy a gift for each other and love that particular giving aspect of our Christmas.

TITHING AND MATH

- Practicing tithing introduces percentages into your child's vocabulary. Ten percent is easy to learn, and from there it makes an easy base and connection to the world of percentages.
- A 20% tip is 10% doubled (more on this in the Mathematics section under "Math in Public").

CASH ENVELOPE SYSTEM

An easy way to start teaching your children how to divide and manage their money is through an envelope system. Cold, hard cash is a good visual for seeing their money grow and dwindle.

Begin this with them as young as 4-5 years old. Include them in the process of separating out their money. I divided their money into predetermined amounts and placed that money in separate envelopes.

For starters, we divided the money into four envelopes: tithe, short-term savings, long-term savings, and spending. Bear in mind what the child's interests are, what they want to save for, and how long it will take to do so.

Here is how I first broke the percentages down:

- 10% tithe
- 20% long term saving (LTS)
- 30% short term saving (STS)
- 40% spending

I initially put a larger chunk into the spending envelope, as I wanted to encourage them. It is hard work to earn money and I didn't pay top dollar. They needed a measure of spending money to stay motivated and make the wait for the savings worth it. As they got older and made more money, I included more guidelines regarding the types of items that could be purchased with their savings, placing more responsibility on them for how they handled their spending envelope.

In the beginning, the requirements to access the short- and long-term envelopes were short, sweet, and simple. They could save for things like a desired toy or towards a planned vacation. Short term was generally reached in 1-3 months, and long term was attained within 3-6 months. Remember, this is a long time to a young child.

As they got older, the envelopes became more developed and specific towards each child's needs and interests. I would write a list of approved expenditures on the LTS and STS envelopes. These envelopes could not be accessed until they reached a predetermined point, and they couldn't be used for any sudden "needs" or flights of fancy. As they made more money, more "wants" had to be bought from their spending money, not with their savings.

DEBT

I dislike debt. My desire was for my children to appreciate the seriousness of debt, make wise decisions, and be good stewards of their finances. I wanted them to understand the consequences and pain of debt at a young age so they would be less likely to repeat those decisions later in life.

While we lived in South Korea, the opportunity arose for learning about personal debt. The two youngest children were seven. They understood the value of money so they were ready to experience the pain of not having money. The destruction of property had occurred, and I charged them for the items that I had to buy.

They each received money for helping out around the house beyond their regular chores. We went through their finances every weekend. However, this time as we went through their finances, they didn't receive their normal spending money. Their tithe, STS, and LTS envelopes received their portions, but all the spending money went towards the debt. Ouch. That hurt.

As the weeks went by, they quickly concluded that they hated debt. When the debt envelope reached the amount they owed, it was with great relief that they began to have spending money again. They also learned to be more careful with others' property.

Though they could not grasp the concept completely, I explained that in real life there is also a concept called interest. I briefly showed them what that would look like, how it added to the amount they owed. I used 10% to make it easy math. It was like adding the tithe every week to the amount they owed. Yuck. They didn't like that.

This was not a one-time deal. Periodically, and especially as they got older, I used money consequences for actions, decisions, and things that got broken. Their spending money was theirs to decide when and how they spent it, unless they had "debt." Then, there was no choice. They had to satisfy the debt out of their spending money.

If they couldn't pay it off one week, it carried over to the next. It was a great motivator, especially when little else mattered to a child and money spoke the loudest. Isn't this true in the adult world as well!

EARLY SAVINGS AND INVESTMENTS

Open a savings account or long-term investment account with your child. They need to be aware that this is money they cannot access or spend. It will be set aside to grow for them. A good time to introduce this is when they receive a chunk of money that is more than they need for their envelopes, like excess birthday and Christmas money. If you have already opened an account with their baby money, then you just need to pull out the documents and show them how their money is growing for them.

Motivate and encourage them to continue adding to their account on a regular basis. They can even use a new envelope to save towards an annual or biannual deposit. Show them how interest works *for* them in this manner, not against them like debt does.

SCIENCE, BIOLOGY, & HEALTH

TIPS:

- Introduce your science topics from life around the home. Science and biology are all about life and life is all around you. It's easy to make meaningful connections for learning.
- Include elements from flowers to clouds to rocks; from animals to birds to crickets; from babies to bathing to body parts; from breathing to digestion to skin healing.
- If you don't know the information offhand, a quick Google search will yield plenty of information.

EXPERIMENTS

Do experiments together. Get a science book from the library and do some projects in it. Or go online to find some to do. Tweak it to fit your schedule and child's interests. Watch YouTube demonstrations and how-to videos for just about anything. After working with hands-on science, the schoolbook will hold more interest and can be used as a review tool.

WEATHER EXAMPLE

We studied the clouds together. I commented on cloud shapes and types as we were driving in the van. I share about this in Chapter 7—How to Create Interest in Learning, under "I Wonder as I Wander."

I led their interest toward forecasting by pondering, "I wonder if one can know when it's going to rain by the kinds of clouds in the sky? I wonder how the weatherman knows." I recounted the old line, "'Red at night, sailor's delight; Red in the morning, sailors take warning.' Do you think that's true? Let's watch the clouds tonight!"

We studied different types and shapes of clouds. Then we made a chart and tracked the clouds and weather. We became amateur "weather forecasters" as we took what we learned and guessed what weather was coming. What would the day likely hold? Sun, rain, or storm? Were they cirrus or cumulus clouds for good weather, or stratus or cumulonimbus clouds ushering in rain or a thunderstorm?

Kids love using new language and vocabulary in this manner. As more questions pop up, they research to find the answers. They are sleuths, scouts, and investigators.

FLOWERS AND PLANTS

- Explain the germination process as you plant flowers and plants in the spring.
- Do some indoor planting so they can watch the process.
    - Plant two egg cartons of seeds—one to watch grow and transplant outside, and the other to use for learning.
    - Dig up a "learning" seed every couple days to see what's happening underground and to follow the germination and growth process.
- Divide and replant clumps of perennial flowers.
    - Show how flowers multiply.
    - Teach the differences between annual, biennial, and perennial plants.

- Learn some plant names.
    - Identify plants along the side of the road or while taking a walk by a creek.
    - Make a bouquet of flowers or plants.
- Plant a tree.
    - If you need to cut down a tree, use that occurence to teach about how trees grow, how to tell the age by the rings inside, and if it is a hardwood or softwood tree.
- How can you tell a plant or tree by its leaves?
    - Collect leaves.
    - Label each type leaf.

ROCKS

- Be on the lookout for unique or unusual rocks.
    - Pick them up, point them out, and wonder aloud about them.
    - Learn the different types of rocks from igneous, sedimentary, and metamorphic.
    - Gather and label a collection of rocks.
    - Take a hike to look for certain rocks or to add to your collection.
    - Lead in to the earth's surface and earth science.

BIRDS

- Go bird watching.
- Go to a nature shelter or habitat.

- Watch for birds along the side of the road.
- Look for birds in the skies.
  - Easy ones to start with are geese during the spring and fall as they migrate.
  - Explain about migration.
- Fun fact: many birds eat up to twice their weight each day.
  - What do they eat?
- Not all birds fly.
  - What's the smallest bird?
  - What's the largest bird?

ANIMALS, INSECTS, AND OCEAN

- Visit a zoo or a farm.
  - If you live on a farm, you've got a head start in this area.
- Find out what animals your children are interested in—start there.
  - Learn about nocturnal versus diurnal.
  - Identify carnivores, herbivores, and detritivores.
  - Which are vertebrates versus invertebrates?
  - Learn about mammals, amphibians, reptiles, fish.
- Proceed to the library or online to learn more about them in depth.
- Learn something new about an ordinary animal.
- Learn about a little-known animal.
- There are over a million species of animals on earth, so you have plenty to choose from!

- Did you know a starfish is not a fish at all?
  - They have no brain or blood, and their stomach comes out their mouth to digest their food.
  - If cut up, they regenerate and grow back their missing arms.
  - What's not to be interesting in this?
- Point out fun biology facts like:
  - An earthworm has five hearts.
  - A cow has four stomachs.
  - Wouldn't it be terrible to be a cow and have *four* tummy aches?

BABIES, BODIES, AND BIOLOGY

Take the opportunity to teach your older children about baby-care and needs while you take care of your little ones.

As they grow, and especially as they have complaints, use these opportunities to learn about that particular area or operation of the body. They hold more interest when they themselves are experiencing something with it.

- Tooth falling out
  - Baby vs permanent teeth
  - Tooth health
  - Hygiene
  - How does a cavity form?

- Sore throat, cough, or cold
  - Virus and bacteria
  - Infections
  - Roles of immune, lymphatic, and respiratory systems
  - Eating healthy
  - Importance of exercise and sleep
- Stubbed toe
  - Nervous system and response to pain
  - Why rubbing the stubbed toe helps mask the hurt
- Cuts, scrapes, burns, and bruises
  - Blood and blood vessels
  - Circulatory system
  - Skin layers
  - Integumentary system
  - The healing process
- Tummy ache, diarrhea, constipation
  - Digestive system
  - Urinary and excretory systems
- Sore muscles, sprains, broken bones
  - How does our body move?
  - Skeletal system
  - Muscular system
  - Nervous system

HISTORY, GEOGRAPHY, & ECONOMICS

TIPS:

- Instead of plugging away systematically through a textbook, pick and choose when you introduce a topic according to their interest and aptitude.
- Dive more deeply into areas of interest.
- Choose something together that you and your child (or all your children) have a collective interest in.
- Offer 2-3 options to choose from.
- Do the research together and learn together.

WORLDWIDE: VIRTUAL VISITS AROUND THE WORLD

- Pick a place they'd like to travel or visit.
    - Learn about that country: where it is in the world, the people, the culture.
    - Their time zone, what they eat, how they work, play, and sleep.
    - Their customs, traditions, clothing, language, festivals, and beliefs.
    - The history of their nation and country, past wars and why.
- Learn a few main words in that language and insert into your daily use.
    - Hello, good morning, please, thank you, goodbye.
    - This is a lot of fun!

- Get books from the library and watch online videos.
- Create a poster or project about the country.
- Visit an ethnic grocery store if available in your area.
- Plan an evening:
    - Make a meal and invite friends over.
    - Share the poster board projects and things you've learned about this country or people group.
- Have your child practice presentation skills:
    - Smiling and making eye contact
    - Speaking with confidence
    - Engaging the audience

NATIONAL: STUDYING THE UNITED STATES

For local studies, you can follow the same pattern as outlined above. Just pick a state to study, then learn about it and its residents.

- A state research
    - State symbols, emblems, and icons such as its seal, flag, capitol, colors, motto, nickname, slogan, and song.
    - State flower, bird, tree, animal, river, insect, fish, and stone/rock.
- States can have fun things to research:
    - A state father, poem, holiday, team, artifact, award, sport, museum, aircraft, rifle, reptile, mineral, fossil, and soil.
    - Even a state exercise, snack, pie, beverage, dance, nut, mushroom, and microbe!

HISTORY, GEOGRAPHY, & ECONOMICS

- Learn about the history of that state:
    - Its time zone
    - When it joined the USA
    - What it is known for
- Learn a few fun facts about it:
    - Famous people, events, wars
    - Geographical sites, national parks, and recreational areas
- Learn about the accents and food preferences of different parts of the country
    - Make a meal or dish with those foods.
- Can you guess which area of the country eats the following collection of foods?
    - Biscuits and gravy, fried green tomatoes, and sorghum
    - Clam chowder, cheesecake, and corned beef
    - Barbeque, chili, and queso
    - Street tacos, garlic fries, and smoked salmon
    - Beer brats, cheese curds, and pickle barrel sandwiches
    - T-bone steak, green chile cheeseburger, and jalapeno and cilantro soup
- Learn about what each state offers
    - Careers and job opportunities
    - Programs, arts, and festivals
- What are the locals called?
    - Who are the Hoosiers, Crackers, Down Easters?
    - The Sooners, Nutmeggers, Bay Staters, and Sandlappers?

- Make a poster or chart with some of these interesting facts about each state as you study them.

LOCAL: HOME ECONOMICS

Now often referred to as Family and Consumer Sciences, this subject focuses on the home and family. The goal is to teach applicable/pertinent life skills and to prepare your child to meet life's opportunities and challenges. To promote health and well-being in all areas. To set your child up to succeed and thrive. To be arrows in the hand of a mighty warrior. (Ps 127:4)

Ultimately, that is what this book is all about … preparing our children to launch strong and hit the target by fulfilling the purpose they were created for. All scholastic and academic learning play into this single goal.

I've already shared several areas of this topic in the book already, which I will refer to.

- Clothing and Household Purchasing
    - Shop and get your child involved with the process
    - See Mathematics, under "Math in Public"
- Kitchen (the purchase, preparation, and service of food)
    - How to start your children helping in the kitchen at an early age:
    - Chapter 3—Raising Responsible Learners, under "The Gift of Work" and "Precept Upon Precept"
    - Chapter 7—How to Create Interest for Learning, under "Practice in Real Life"

- How to begin the shopping process with your children at an early age:
  - Chapter 7—How to Create Interest for Learning, under "Invest Early."
- A great example:
  - Chapter 3—Raising Responsible Learners, under "James' 7th Birthday Supper."

MORE KITCHEN IDEAS

Meal Planning

- Go through the fridge, freezer, and cupboard foods together.
- See what needs to be eaten and what meal can be made.
- Write a list of meals to make.
- Use a recipe book or go online to search out meals (look for a dish that uses a particular leftover or ingredient).
- Make a list of ingredients that are needed for those meals.

Grocery Lists

- Include your child when compiling your grocery list.
- If you base it off meals for the week, then ask for their input or show them the recipes you'll be using and go through the list of ingredients together.
- As you read off ingredients, have them check the fridge and cupboards to see what you have and what needs to go on the list.
- At the store, include them in helping check off the list.

Deal Shopping and Budgeting

- Check store ads: which store has the better deal on what?
- Food price comparison: show them how to check the price or do the math to get the best price per oz/lb/item.
- Show them your target dollar amount and see how close you can stay within that range.
- Utilize coupons: paper and digital.

HOME AND VEHICLE MAINTENANCE

Kids hold a glorified view of all things adult. They point out the biggest and nicest house they want to live in someday. Every boy imagines the fastest and coolest car he'll drive, and every girl daydreams about her perfect Prince Charming and their babies.

It is good for children to realize the work that goes into a family and home maintenance. It is also good for them to gain skills in a variety of areas. This helps them define what they enjoy doing and what they need to practice.

Household

- Measure, plan, and rearrange furniture together.
- Have them help with projects around the house.
- Fix a leaky faucet, clean out a clogged drain, change a light bulb.
- Plumbing, electrical, carpentry, mechanical, painting.
- Include them in tasks, even if holding a flashlight or handing you tools.

Siblings

- Give them oversight responsibilities.
- Watch over the baby or younger siblings.
- Work in pairs or partnership with a sibling.
- Work together to figure out a problem.

Computer and Electronics

- Find old electronics at garage sales and let them work on them.
- Try to fix something, try to take something apart and put it back together, try to rebuild something or overhaul it.

Outdoors

- Feed and water animals/pets.
- Plan, plant, upkeep, and harvest their own little portion of garden.
- Choose and plant a small flower bed.
- Mow and trim the lawn.

Vehicles

- Wash, clean out, sweep, and detail.
- Check and add oil and fluids.
- Change a lightbulb.
- If you work on vehicles, let the child pass tools to you and assist as you work under the hood.

SCRIPTURE: STUDY & MEMORIZATION

TIPS:

- Take as active of a role in teaching your child about God as you do in their secular studies. God entrusted you with this task and honor.
- All of nature reflects the goodness and character of God and teaches us something about Him.
- Take the time to point out connections as you see them, and teach your children to look for the connections between the spiritual and the natural.

BIBLE AND DAILY LIFE

Let nature instruct and be a reminder of God and His ways. I would often point out things like God's love for beauty (flowers, mountains, ocean, etc.), and how He creates things bigger than we can imagine, yet smaller than we can see (astronomic vs microscopic).

- When we came across a dead bird, I'd remind them that God's eye is on the sparrow, and He knew this little birdie had died.
- When we picked flowers, I'd mention how beautifully God took care of them, and how much more He takes care of us.
- When a hair would fall out when I brushed their hair, I'd comment that God had to subtract that hair from their total hair count, and I wondered what that number was now. Only He knew, because I sure didn't want to count them!

BIBLE AND ACADEMICS

The Bible holds a lot of literary value.

- Includes three of four literary genres:
    - poetry, nonfiction, and drama
- Literary forms:
    - historical, law, wisdom, poetry, prophecy, apocalyptic, and gospel
- The Bible also includes beautiful and captivating figurative language.
- Use the Bible and integrate it into their other subjects.

Literature

- Study a book, character, or topic from the Bible.
- Learn about the truth, authority, person and reflection of God in the account.
- Study a Proverb and the timeless truths it imparts.
- Study the songs in the Bible (examples: Miriam, Moses, Deborah, David, Solomon).

English and Pronunciation

- Study the tower of Babel.
- Study the old English style from King James Version.
- Practice reading names and places from the Old Testament, using the pronunciation key found in the front of the Bible.

Math

- Learn math terms, like "score."
- Practice writing out numbers from written form, like from Genesis 5.

Science

- Study Genesis and the creation account. Discuss what the Bible says about the origin of life versus other theories, like evolution.
- Study Noah's flood. How fossils were formed afterwards and how the flood affected the earth. The difference in weather before and after the flood. The effect on life span as a result.
- Discuss miracles and faith from a biblical viewpoint. How they play into our lives even today.
- Teach your children to be Berean (Acts 17:11) and examine what they hear against Scripture.
- Answers in Genesis is a great resource for understanding the Bible and science.

History and Social Studies

- After reading a story, reflect how people acted then and how we do now.
  - What have we learned?
  - Do we make the same mistakes?
  - What were some of their customs?
  - How do they differ from today?
  - How are they similar?

SCRIPTURE: STUDY & MEMORIZATION

Geography

- Track Israel's journey from Egypt to the Promised Land.
- Make a map of Israel.
- Track Jesus' travels in the Gospels.
- Track the Apostle Paul's journey in Acts.

Art and Music:

- Coloring in Bible story coloring books.
- Drawing a scene from a Bible story.
- Drawing or coloring as you read them a Bible story.
- Listen to Bible songs while coloring and drawing.
- Put a psalm to music.
- Sing a psalm.
- Sing songs based on Bible verses.

Speech and Drama

- We shared our stance of "God said it, I believe it, and that settles it." We would demonstrate and show our children how to read and speak out God's word.
- Demonstrate reading aloud from the Bible with an authority that honors the words you are reading. It is our truth and authority, so it must be read as such.
- Teach them how to speak clearly:
    - Opening their mouth bigger
    - Over-articulating the words

- Quote Scripture verses or read from the Bible around the table. It's a great way to practice speaking with authority and confidence.
- Younger ones take turns reading a verse aloud.
- Older ones take turns reading a Psalm or Proverb.

SCRIPTURE MEMORIZATION & DELIVERY

Scripture memorization is powerful, especially while the children are young. Growing up, we would learn verses as a family, reciting a verse together each mealtime until we had it memorized, usually one a week. We also memorized the "ABC Verses," a verse starting with each letter. We performed at a homeschool talent show one year, taking turns quoting through the verses.

Talking about the verse being memorized is helpful in digesting and understanding it. It is important to learn the message of the verse, not have sheer memorization. Then the verse can be applied to parenting and for instruction with greater impact and meaning.

BIBLE READING

A wonderful Bible application for reading the Bible through in a year is called "Read Scripture." It is a free app and includes short videos giving an overview of each book as you read through them. I love it! Also called "The Bible Project," they have a growing website of Bible studies to get you started or take you deeper into a topic.

Each day's reading is broken down into a daily reading plus a Psalm. You can follow the reading plan and then read out of your own Bible. They do include the daily reading in the app, however this reading is currently only offered in one Bible version. I recommend reading from your Bible to decrease screen time on your eyes.

You can access Read Scripture's website through www.readscripture.org.

WORKS CITED

CHAPTER 2

1. Curwood, Jen. "What Happened to Kindergarten?" *scholastic.com,* (n.d.) https://www.scholastic.com/teachers/articles/teaching-content/what-happened-kindergarten/. Accessed 25 October 2019.

2. Helliwell, John et al. "World Happiness Report 2018." *World Happiness Report,* 14 March 2018, https://worldhappiness.report/ed/2018/. Accessed 25 October 2019.

3. Sanchez, Claudio. "What the U.S. Can Learn from Finland, Where School Starts At Age 7." *npr.org,* 08 March 2014, https://www.npr.org/2014/03/08/287255411/what-the-u-s-can-learn-from-finland-where-school-starts-at-age-7. Accessed 25 October 2019.

4. Programme for International Student Assessment. "PISA 2015: Results in Focus" 2018, *oecd.org* https://www.oecd.org/pisa/pisa-2015-results-in-focus.pdf. Accessed 25 October 2019.

5. Walker, Timothy. "How Finland Keeps Kids Focused Through Free Play." *The Atlantic*, 30 June 2014, https://www.theatlantic.com/education/archive/2014/06/how-finland-keeps-kids-focused/373544/. Accessed 25 October 2019.

6. Hancock, LynNell. "Why Are Finland's Schools Successful?" *smithsonianmag.com*, September 2011. https://www.smithsonianmag.com/innovation/why-are-finlands-schools-successful-49859555/. Accessed 21 October 2019.

7. Butler, Patrick. "No grammar schools, lots of play: the secrets of Europe's top education system." *theguardian.com*, 20 September 2016, https://www.theguardian.com/education/2016/sep/20/grammar-schools-play-europe-top-education-system-finland-daycare. Accessed 25 October 2019.

8. Walker, Timothy. "How Finland Starts the School Year." *The Atlantic*, 25 August 2016, https://www.theatlantic.com/education/archive/2016/08/how-finland-starts-the-school-year/497306/. Accessed 25 October 2019.

9. University of Otago. "Late readers close learning gap." *Science Alert*, 03 January 2010, https://www.sciencealert.com/late-readers-close-learning-gap. Accessed 25 October 2019.

CHAPTER 5

1. Buhler, Rich et al. "After a Schoolteacher Called Thomas Edison "Addled," His Heroic Mother Stepped In—Mostly Fiction." *truthorfiction.com,* 05 October 2015. https://www.truthorfiction.com/after-a-schoolteacher-called-thomas-edison-addled-his-heroic-mother-stepped-in/. Accessed 1 November 2019.

2. "Overview of Learning Styles." *learning-styles-online.com,* (n.d.), https://www.learning-styles-online.com/overview/. Accessed 19 November 2019

3. Haralabidou, Anastasia. "The philosophy of epic entrepreneurs: Thomas Edison & the Vagabonds." *virgin.com,* 14 October 2015, https://www.virgin.com/entrepreneur/philosophy-epic-entrepreneurs-thomas-edison-vagabonds. Accessed 1 November 2019

ABOUT THE AUTHOR

Wanda Kinsinger is a wife, mother, author, and communicator who was privileged with the opportunity of being both a homeschool kid and a homeschool mom. She was part of the pioneer homeschool movement in the 1980s. After three years at a small country public school, she was homeschooled from third grade through high school. She graduated a year early and earned her associates degree in physical therapy.

After getting married, Wanda and her husband adopted three children from Vietnam and chose to homeschool them. Two of the children graduated early and, as young adults, all three are pursuing their respective dream careers in neurosurgery, software development, and business. With an emptying nest and as a committed life-long learner, Wanda is pursuing continued education with a focus in the developmental years.

Now Wanda's mission is to share her experiences with other young mothers to encourage and support them along their homeschool journey. She believes that any mother can homeschool, and seeks to provide practical advice, encouragement, and creative teaching to set children up to thrive and succeed. Her goal is to equip young mothers to prepare their children to launch strong and fulfill the purpose and destiny God created them for.

If your area hosts a homeschool conference or would be interested in inviting the author to speak, please contact for requests:

wandakinsinger.com
FB: @wandakinsinger
Instagram: @wandakinsinger
Twitter: @wandakinsinger